Redeeming the Routines:
Bringing Theology to Life

A BRIDGEPOINT BOOK

BridgePoint,
the academic
imprint of
Victor Books, is
your connection
for the best in
serious reading
that integrates
the passion of
the heart with
the scholarship
of the mind.

REDEEMING THE ROUTINES

BRINGING THEOLOGY TO LIFE

ROBERT BANKS

A
BRIDGEPOINT
BOOK

All Scripture quotations are from the *Revised Standard Version of the Bible,* © 1946, 1952, 1971, 1973.

Copyediting: Robert N. Hosack
Cover Design: Scott Rattray

Library of Congress Cataloging-in-Publication Data

Banks, Robert J.
    Redeeming the routines: bringing theology to life /
Robert Banks.
        p.   cm.
    Includes bibliographical references.
    ISBN 1-56476-077-4
    1. Christian life—1960-   2. Theology.   I. Title.
BV4501.2.B3824   1993
240–dc20   92-41788
                                                      CIP

---

1 2 3 4 5 6 7 8 9 10 Printing / Year 97 96 95 94 93

BridgePoint is the academic imprint of Victor Books.

CONTENTS

FOREWORD

When you want something done right, go to the professional. This watchword of specialization is true as a general rule. But there is one area where our love affair with the specialist has not served us well: the study and practice of theology. Not that professional theologians do not exist. They are to be found in every seminary and most Christian colleges, but there is a growing sense that they serve a shrinking, some would say nonexistent, market. What is worse there appears to be a growing gulf between professional theologians and what we call—sometimes disparaging—ordinary Christians. I still remember the shock I felt as a seminarian when an older friend of mine, who served on the faculty of a Lutheran seminary, introduced himself to someone as a "theologian." What, I wondered, does a theologian "do"? Years later, though I have gotten used to people calling me a theologian, I still wonder: what purpose do we serve?

It is true that theology has developed all the trappings of a profession. We have our own scholarly journals, professional associations, and even a common credentialing process.[1] What's more one can actually make a living writing for these journals, teaching theology, and attending conferences. It is also true that this "profession" requires mastery of a growing number of subspecialities—not only languages, history, philosophy, and practical disciplines like preaching and counseling, but increasingly sophisticated areas of social and literary theory. One certainly would not want to argue that these have no value to Christians outside the academy.

But just at this point the uniqueness of Christian theology becomes apparent. There is a sense in which the very purpose of theology is to be found in the lives of people outside the profession of theology, in a way very different from, say, medicine or law. This has been true from the very beginning of the church. In the first century the Apostle Paul said of the believers: "You show that you are a letter from Christ delivered by us, written not with ink but with the Spirit of the living God . . . on tablets of human hearts" (2 Cor. 3:3). This vision of what we might call "lay theol-

---

[1]For a valuable study of the development of this professionalism see D.G. Hart, "The Troubled Soul of the Academic: American Learning and the Problem of Religious Studies," *Religion and American Culture: A Journal of Interpretation* (Winter 1992): 49-77.

ogy" fired the reformers of the sixteenth century who recaptured the New Testament notion of the "priesthood of all believers." On this view theology is actually formulated by all believers as they follow Christ's leading in their work and families or as they give witness to the Gospel in their neighborhood. The role professional theologians play in all this—unlike professionals in other fields—is supportive and tentative, rather than central and definitive. Unlike other areas of life, the experts here are more often than not those with no formal training—think of those we used to call "soul winners" or "prayer warriors."

While this way of thinking has a long history and, from a biblical point of view, seems quite normal, it still unfortunately sounds radical to many Christians (and especially to their teachers and preachers). Theologians sometimes feel threatened by thoughtful laity; laypeople often feel unprepared for the challenges they face. But the vision is far from dead as Robert Banks amply demonstrates in this lucid and thoughtful book. In these pages he connects with the tradition of lay theology, in Scripture and history, which I referred to above. There he finds ample resources for Christians to apply to their workplaces and communities. But more than that, he shows the theological significance of the issues that believers struggle with day by day: work, family, leisure, eating, and sleeping. One might argue in fact that the major theological questions we face at the end of our century come to special focus in the daily living which is the theme of Banks' study.

Here is a theologian who is working to close the gap between theology and the people of God. Already, as a result of thinkers like Banks, there is indication in the profession itself that academics are learning to reread Scripture with the new eyes that everyday living gives them—just as Latin American theologians have taught us to reread the Bible from the point of view of those suffering oppression. What this might mean for a fresh biblical studies paradigm is hinted at in these pages. But even more important is the way this study challenges God's people in every setting to "live unto God"—as the Puritan William Ames put it. For if all of us can begin to see the whole of life lived in the presence and by the power of God, theology and everyday life will have met and embraced. May God use this book to bring that day nearer.

WILLIAM A. DYRNESS

PREFACE

In some respects this book has its roots in questions I began to ask during the sixties about the status and role of ordinary Christians. At that time I was involved in pastoral work in a large city church in Australia and later in a small working class parish in England. Part of my concern stemmed from the way ordinary Christians were often marginalized in the church yet also isolated from the world at large. Wrestling with these issues gradually led to a significant revising of my understanding of both church and ministry.

During some of this time I was also completing doctoral work in biblical studies. As that was coming to an end, increasingly I came to feel that I was in a theological ghetto myself, divorced from what was happening in the wider intellectual and social world. In order to close the distance between these, I decided to withdraw from church-related work and spent the next ten years in a secular university environment.

Unexpectedly I gained a five-year position in a research school of social sciences and was able to work on some of the key figures and movements that have shaped contemporary attitudes and structures. This was followed by a five-year teaching position in a history department at another university. There I became more and more interested in the everyday first-century setting of the ideas and activities of the earliest Christians—economic, social, political, and cultural—and in the rise and impact of the main secular world-views and movements on contemporary life over the last two centuries.

In both these places, my wife and I began to discover a more communal and down-to-earth church life. In these house churches — or basic Christians communities as they are called in some parts of the world—I saw first hand the enormous capacity all Christians have for engaging in mutual ministry. I also learned how they were able to work through many of their everyday concerns, dilemmas, and responsibilities.

It was during this time that I wrote about Paul's idea of community, hoping to alert Christians to the challenge of Paul's highly participatory and down-to-earth view of the church. For him, church was essentially a people's affair and everyone had a vital part to play in every aspect of its life. To his mind, church was also about everyday concerns as much as anything else and this gave to the gatherings a highly practical air. Turning these ideas into a more popular format persuaded me that any attempt at "bringing theology to life" had to have as great a concern for form as for content.

About this time, some ten years ago now, I was browsing through a bookstore and came across a copy of Freud's work, *The Psychopathology of Everyday Life*. The reference to everyday life in Freud's title reminded me of Baillie's address on the theology of sleep that my wife and I had read almost fifteen years before. Then and there it occurred to me that what we needed was a wide-ranging "theology of everyday life," one that would give a sustained attention to the issues of daily living as to the traditional subjects of theological reflection.

A year or two later, while on sabbatical, it became clear that we faced a change of direction. So we entered into a more independent existence, one rooted in the house churches with which we had been involved and linked with certain interdenominational organizations attempting more generally to relate Christianity to Australian society. These commitments and interests have continued, only now focused in a North American context since our move to the United States.

What form does this way of life take? Sometimes my work is with occupational or student groups who are trying to work out how their faith should affect the work they are doing or preparing for and the institutions in which they are or will be doing it. Where such groups are made up of students, this involves alerting them to the vocational responsibilities and dilemmas that one day they are going to face. Sometimes I am in the company of people hovering between belief and unbelief, many of whose dilemmas I find arise from their practical experience of life rather than intellectual objections.

My wife and I also spend time with groups of people who wish to identify, work through, and confront some of the pervasive forces that shape so much of our daily lives. Many people feel oppressed by—and are looking for a Christian perspective upon—the pressures of time, change, and mobility or feel powerless in the face of bureaucratic regulation or professional takeover of many parts of their lives. They wish to be liberated from these and indeed it is powers such as these, along with others relevant to more disadvantaged groups in our society, that should provide the agenda of a theology of liberation for our own context. Frequently, together with others, we give extended time to congregations and other Christian groups, encouraging them to develop their full potential for mutual ministry and support and suggesting how they might better relate their faith to all the areas of life in which they are engaged.

Most of the writing I have done over the past ten years has its basis in one or other of the activities I have mentioned. A symposium on private values and public policy arose out of a four-year working group made up of senior public servants. We sought to discover how far fundamental Christian beliefs should or could inform decision-making in government administration. Writing about the tyranny of time had its origins in the problems my family and others had in this area; meanwhile, a book on developing house churches today, written together with my wife, was an extension of our efforts to help congregations and individuals establish such groups so that all believers might be able to take greater responsibility for their Christian nurture and mission.

Over those years we were also grappling with an underlying issue. If all Christians have a responsibility to bring their deepest convictions into contact with their most everyday concerns, what are the most effective ways of doing this? Are the learning structures in our congregations, parachurch groups, colleges, and seminaries equipping us adequately? This issue came to a head for me toward the end of the eighties. Over the previous few years I had developed links with a number of new lay educational institutions in North America, England, and Europe. In varying degrees, these institutions suggested ways in which it was possible to reshape the content and methods of theological education to reach a broader audience. In achieving this, these places began to show congregations and Christian organizations how they could reshape their adult learning programs. A description of the most important of these institutions is provided in Appendix A.

What was not clear was whether more traditional theological institutions, such as seminaries, could find more than token room for lay theological concerns. On the basis of what I had observed and conversations I had held, I had serious doubts about this. A consultation with members of Fuller Theological Seminary in the mid-eighties, though, began to change my mind about these matters. Through the vision of a group of ordinary Christians who wished to see "lay ministry" at the center of what the seminary was doing, and the commitment of the administration to realize this vision, a decision was made to establish a department along these lines.

Much to my surprise, three years later I found myself setting up this very department. Moving to Los Angeles at the end of the eighties opened up a fresh chapter in the quest to bring theology into closer contact with ordinary people and with everyday life. In the midst of this I have continued to work with occupational groups, at present with members of the film and television industry in Hollywood. My wife and I continue to develop basic Christian communities or house churches in our region, both within the seminary and in congregations. I also remain committed to creating resources for ordinary Christians in the church and workplace.

For those who are interested in such matters, the way in which the concerns of this book have been worked out within the seminary itself—at the level of curriculum, program, and classroom—is also briefly described in Appendix A. This raises the further question of how much the seminary context is open to not only making room for the concerns of ordinary Christians, but to examining afresh the goals, methods, and teaching of theology from the perspective of the people.

This book owes much to the contributions of others. Through various conversations and letters, I am indebted to Peter Marshall, Stephen Barton, and Bill Dyrness—in Australia, England, and North America—for the ideas and clarifications they offered. An earlier version was read, and extensively commented on, by David Millikan, Lynlea Rodger, and Andrew Hingeley, and their suggestions helped me to reshape some of the material. I am grateful to Gwen Garrison, who provided one of the case studies that appear in chapter 1, and to Ed White, Jr., who supplied some of the information in Appendix B. Initially Ken Goodlet, and recently Robert Hosack, have applied their editorial skills to improving the manuscript. But I also owe much to countless ordinary Christians, from whom I have learned so much over the years in various settings where these issues have been discussed. Without their contributions and general encouragement this book, such as it is, would not have come into being.

ONE
Setting the Scene

Almost twenty-five years ago my wife and I were visited by a staff member from the seminary we had recently attended. Having just joined the staff of a large city church in another state, we were pleased to see a well-known face. To thank us for our hospitality, he left us a book called *Christian Devotion* by a well-known Scottish author, John Baillie, which contained a chapter with the unusual title "A Theology of Sleep." Was this a serious title or was the writer just catching our attention? After quoting Psalm 127:1-2, he introduced the subject in the following way:

> My subject is the theology of sleep. It is an unusual subject, but I make no apology for it. I think we hear far too few sermons about sleep. After all, we spend a very large share of our lives sleeping. I suppose that on average I've slept for eight hours out of every twenty-four during the whole of my life, and that means I've slept for well over twenty years. . . . Don't you agree then that the Christian gospel should have something to say about the sleeping third of our lives as well as about the waking two-thirds of them? I believe it has something to say and that this text serves as a good beginning for the exposition of it.[1]

Baillie's juxtaposition of "theology" with something as mundane as "sleep" came as a shock. Theology only dealt with those lofty themes arising out of God's plan of salvation. How could so routine—and unconscious—an activity as sleep have anything to do with it? But the more I thought about it the more I was convinced. Did not the Bible encourage us to view all our activities and responsibilities in the light of Christ? If so, then it was proper to preach and teach on such a matter. And if it was proper to do this, then theology should help clarify what should be said.

At the time I did not see the implications of what Baillie was saying for systematic Christian thinking and *redeeming the routines* of life. If there was some link between believing and sleeping, then I should start connecting up my basic convictions with many other areas of life that I had previously taken for granted. While I had long believed in principle that Christianity should affect the whole of one's life, I had not appreciated how wide-ranging or deep-thinking an obligation that was. Nor did I sense at the time that Baillie's remarks might lead to further questions about the whole enterprise of theology. In fact, so pressured was our life during our time at the city church that I was not even able to put into practice what he said about sleeping!

I would not claim to see the full implications of what he was saying even now. But gradually I have become aware of what some of those are. This was not a purely intellectual affair: only as I listened to others' difficulties and worked through some personal dilemmas did I begin to appreciate what was involved.

Scenes from Everyday Life

To explain the practical outworkings of this basic insight, it is appropriate to start with some stories rather than statements. The Bible itself, the basis of the Christian faith, is largely a series of stories. Much of its relevance comes from that. The best stories, whether personal ones or those of other people, have a way of focusing on the issue. We also tend to identify with them more easily. I begin with several stories told to me by people I know. These people are by no means untypical. I follow their stories with part of my own, since this explains what led me to write this book.

The following stories occurred in a relatively short space of time to people who belonged to the same small group. I wish I had taken down their stories verbatim so that I could let them speak in their own words. But even they have difficulty now putting themselves back fully into the situations they described. To protect the anonymity of those involved, I have changed certain details of age, name, and even sex.

1. Chris: A Work-related Problem

I have known Chris for more than ten years. We first met when I was still teaching in a university and he was in his early twenties. A few months after we had moved to Canberra (Australia) we met up again, not socially this time but in a more personal way. Chris is quiet-spoken, but outgoing and a real "people person." He has a good sense of humor and enjoys sports.

He has a degree in economics and works for a large fast-growing computer company. At the time of the particular problem I want to relate he was climbing through the ranks to more responsible positions and had just entered middle-management with a number of people under his supervision. He had not gone out of his way to seek promotions, being content to master each job he had been given and stay in it until his superiors encouraged him to apply for a new situation.

Chris is married to Tammy, a school teacher, who gets home around 3:30 in the afternoon and is therefore able to help more with domestic responsibilities and their young child. The only problem with their dual working patterns stemmed from occasional bouts of sickness Tammy suffered, which sometimes kept her in bed for several days at a time. Chris felt badly when these illnesses came, and he occasionally took time off from work to look after his wife.

Because of the growing volume of work, Chris was under pressure to work longer hours. This placed extra pressure upon Tammy in the home at dinnertime. It also meant less time together. However, others in the firm, and especially his boss, were tending to work even more overtime, all without receiving any additional wages. Chris felt a real responsibility to his section and also felt guilty for not putting in as much time as others. Though it did not rank highly with him, he knew that further promotional prospects were possibly tied to others' estimates of his commitment to the job.

When we discussed the matter Chris admitted that part of the reason for his doing overtime was his attitude toward work. For example, his boss sometimes passed on work to him from senior management that was marked urgent. But he had been in the firm long enough to know that if left for a couple of weeks some of this would become redundant. Yet he found it difficult to engage in deliberate delaying tactics and there was always the chance that he would set aside the wrong item. Chris has always prided himself on doing his work thoroughly, but if he continued to try to do everything asked of him, and do it thoroughly or in time, he would have to remain longer at his desk.

There was a further problem. Chris has always been sensitive to other people's problems and a good listener. Discerning this, some of his colleagues discussed their problems with him from time to time, even the boss. Chris saw these conversations as a real contribution. But giving attention to people in this way left him even less time to finish the work on his desk. In addition, Chris wanted to give more time to the people in his church and found this suffering because of the extra time he had to spend at work.

Chris' dilemma is not uncommon. Put yourself in his shoes and ask what he should do in this situation. With respect to the workweek, should he keep generally to the legal number of hours he was contracted to work or regularly stay longer when things are getting behind? Is his first duty to his wife and daughter? What balance should he seek to achieve between work, family, and church responsibilities, not to speak of sports? Should he yield to the pressure to stay longer at work out of a sense of responsibility to his colleagues or to increase his chances of gaining a more responsible position? How much of the problem is basically the company's rather than his because of the pressures and expectations loaded upon him?

Further, what role should excellence or thoroughness play in his goals? In other words, how Christian are these values or how manipulated are they by employers to their own ends? And how feasible are either of them in the pressured working conditions imposed on most employees? Where thoroughness and deadlines come into conflict, is it better to do everything partially well or only certain things fully well? Should he make it a priority not to jeopardize his chances of promotion so that he can later exercise a greater influence upon the way the company operates? How obligated is Chris to follow all his superior's instructions for example? Should he confront his superior with the tensions he is experiencing and ask for a fairer deal?

More generally, what produces the present work situation

which puts people under such pressure, and should not companies do something about it? Do they not have a responsibility to insure that work remains humane, even at the expense of productivity? How much responsibility do superiors have to work at a pace and length that does not exert pressure upon their subordinates? Should not job descriptions take account of time employees spend on interpersonal matters which may significantly affect both productivity and morale? What is the personal and social cost, even the ultimate economic cost, of energy not spent at home deepening relationships and strengthening family life?

2. Robyn: A Leisure Time Dilemma
Robyn has a love for sports and competition. At a young age she had displayed a natural talent for coordination and had learned the discipline and skill of several different sports. In her college and young adult life she had been fortunate to compete at some high levels. After battling injuries and fatigue she decided to spend her leisure time coaching, giving back to kids what she herself had been able to learn throughout the years. Having worked on and off with different ages, she was offered the opportunity to be on a coaching staff for a high school girls' soccer team. The head coach was confident of her abilities and allowed her the freedom to develop her own program with the younger developing members.

After two very successful seasons and gaining the confidence of the team, she began to experience some difficulty. The members of the upper divisional team were unhappy and morale was low. Their performance on the field lacked respect and teamwork. The talented younger players who had opportunities to practice and compete with the upper level team were frustrated at the lack of coaching and encouragement they were receiving.

During the season several players returned to Robyn's team practices to be in a better environment and to receive more discipline to develop their knowledge and skill of the game. She began experiencing resentment from the head coach, and rumors began to circulate that many of the parents were disappointed in the upper divisional coaching. Robyn resisted contributing to any of the rumors and continued to develop the skills of the younger players.

At the end of the season a huge problem developed. Several of the players in the upper division had seriously violated athletic codes for the team. According to the governing policies these athletes were immediately suspended. The four players involved differed in significance to the team, some being very important players. The news of the problem came on the day of the final match of the season. The upper divisional team had a losing record through a difficult season, and their match that day was against the best team in the division. The lower divisional team was completing another tremendous season and was facing a championship match. Both games were scheduled at the same time and in different locations.

The head coach came to Robyn and asked for the four best players of Robyn's team even though there was enough depth on the upper team to cover all positions and substitutions. Recognizing the tension at that moment and throughout the season, Robyn agreed and went to talk to her players. They balked and did not want to play with the upper level team. Robyn encouraged them to move up, even though she felt disappointed that her whole team would not be present for their final game and a shot at a division title. The players called their parents, asking them to try persuading the coaches to decide otherwise. The parents called the coaches and Robyn was caught in the cross-fire of angry parents, players, and the head coach. Her own feelings of developing a great bunch of players were dissolved in the battle. The teamwork and confidence she had strived to instill in her players was disrupted and lost in the heat of the decision.

What should she do? Side with the parents and players and against the head coach? That could cost her future opportunities to coach in the higher levels. Should she side with the head coach and against her own team members? That could cost her the respect and confidence of her players. What if she kept quiet and allowed the head coach and the parents to work it out? Might her silence communicate that she really didn't care about her players? Would they feel abandoned at a critical time? Would the remaining players resent the actions and let that impede their play for the game?

Who was Robyn primarily responsible to? The players, kids needing support and encouragement in their achievements? The coach, who had recognized her talents and allowed her to develop the program? The parents, whose money and children kept the programs going year after year? Herself, and the standards of teamwork and trust she developed in her players around the skills and knowledge of the game? The moment was agonizing and the fracture of the teams was growing more and more painful. Could there be a fair decision for everyone?

3. Jan: A Role Definition Dilemma

Jan is in her early thirties and has four small children. These were born less than a year apart and the youngest has just turned three. After she completed her university degree, she worked as an interior decorator, mostly advising large companies and businesses on office decor. She was extremely good at her job and was highly regarded by her employers. But during the last seven years, motherhood and housework has been a more than full-time occupation. We have known Jan for nearly fifteen years and my wife in particular has had a lot to do with her. Jan is a very capable person, with independent opinions and an extremely practical approach to life. She is a no-nonsense person and has a strong sense of living by her values.

Ian, her husband, is involved in a small but growing legal practice and has recently been made a partner. Though he has tried to take his family responsibilities seriously, the sudden growth of the company and his new position have made heavy demands upon him. Until the past few months he has resisted any pressures to take work home with him. At times he now finds this difficult to avoid. As a number of his clients have interstate interests, he has to make regular trips to other cities, sometimes being away for two or three nights at a time. He tries to make up for this by keeping holidays scrupulously free and taking long breaks whenever possible.

Allow me to take you back to the situation Jan was in at the time she talked about her dilemma. Some of you will identify with her. Enter into her situation as it was then and consider how you would approach it. Jan has reached the point where the last of the children will begin preschool. She has been entering into a new period of freedom gradually over the last two years and is looking forward to it with considerable anticipation. There are some books she has always wanted to read. There are people with whom she would like to spend more time. There are one or two practical courses she is thinking of taking. She also takes prayer seriously and would like to have more time for it.

There are pressures working against this happening. She still has a lot of housework, shopping, and family coordinating to do which she does not mind greatly, but at times it gets her down. Not only is it repetitive, but when there is sickness in the house, as there frequently seems to be, she has to abandon most of her plans. Ian's regular absences have also put pressure on the free time she is beginning to experience.

A number of her friends who have moved back into the work force assume that she will return to work the moment her youngest child is in preschool. These friends constantly talk about the need to fulfill oneself through meaningful employment. They also point out the greater financial independence this would give her. They tend to regard anyone who stays at home as in danger of becoming a vegetable. Jan feels the pressure of their attitude and wonders whether she will have enough social interaction and intellectual stimulation if she does not go back to work.

There are other factors to consider. While ideally she would prefer to remain at home, almost all her peers in the neighborhood now have jobs. She feels rather lonely at times, particularly when her husband is away. Her friends from church live across town, too far to drop in on in a casual way. Her extended family lives in another city, and in any case relations with some of its members are strained. She does have informal links with a voluntary welfare agency, which would like her to do some unpaid part-time work. But she would have to be careful that this did not surreptitiously claim more time than she wishes to give.

What then should she do? Is it possible to make the nurturing of her children and the deepening of the relationship with her husband her main vocation, yet become fulfilled and liberated in the way she believes a person should be? If so, can she combine this with part-time volunteer work, even though this might intermittently encroach upon time she would like to give to reading, visiting, and taking an occasional course? Although she would meet people by doing some of these things, how does she avoid the problem of loneliness while she is at home? She wonders where she will draw the strength from to resist the pressures of her friends who are employed full-time.

There are other issues. Would the lengthy periods of time she devotes to housework, shopping, and related chores become more satisfying if she could find a deeper purpose in these activities?

How does she handle the fatigue that mothering and domestic work induces, especially in relation to prayer and meditation which often require more energy than she has available? Given the busy-ness of her closest friends, how can she spend enough time with them to maintain and deepen such relationships?

Underlying some of these queries are a number of very serious social issues. For example, what are the main factors eroding rela-tionships in modern society and how can they be combatted? How can cities be planned so as to make suburbs less isolated from the most dynamic centers of their lives? Should companies be obliged to make up time that is taken from families by their employees having to travel on their behalf? How important or feasible is it for churches to restructure themselves so they can develop a degree of neighborliness in the increasingly deserted suburbs of the mod-ern city?

4. Neil and Sue: A Life-stage Decision
I would also like to introduce you to Neil and Sue. We have not known them as long as we have the others, but our links now go back some time. Neil is in his late thirties and comes from a lower middle-class background, as does his wife. They were married in their late teens. The older of their two sons has a job as an apprentice and the younger has left school and is presently unem-ployed. Some years ago they had to move from the city where they were married.

Sue and Neil were both influenced by the counter-culture move-ment in the late sixties and early seventies, before they met as well as afterward. Both had become members of a Christian com-munity and were attracted to the simple lifestyle. Neil had also spent time in a Third World country and was deeply affected by what he encountered. It was shortly after his return that he and Sue met.

Neil and Sue were at a crossroads in their lives. For most of his working life Neil has worked as a projectionist in a theater. The work has not always been regular, the hours are difficult and he has often found his job monotonous. To supplement his income, and to help pay off the mortgage on their home, Sue took a part-time job in a welfare agency. Although they live in an older home in one of the poorer parts of the city, they found they did not have much money to spare.

Outside his employment, Neil loves to work with his hands. He has considerable skill as a potter, but has little time to give to this interest. For a long time he has dreamt about taking up craft as a full-time activity. He knows that such a decision would involve financial struggle for a time, but believes he could eventually make a living from his craftwork. Sue has encouraged both his interest in pottery and dream of an alternative occupation. Secretly, however, she is concerned about their future security, especially as her job with the welfare agency is vulnerable to government cutbacks. She is also aware that Neil would need additional equipment to do his work properly and that it would take some time before he could establish a clientele for his craftwork. Also, if things did not work out, it is clear that once Neil has resigned his projectionist position, there is little likelihood he could regain it.

Any such move raises a number of difficult issues. How much should we expect our employment to be related to our creative capacities? How much should we be willing under God to take risks, both for ourselves and our families, in choosing an occupation? How much should a concern for security be a factor? At what stage in life can major changes of this kind be most effectively made?

There are other questions. What responsibility does the local church have to a person or family in this position? If the church encourages a move in a new direction, does it have an obligation to help out financially until the new line of work is reasonably established? How far should the church be challenging its people generally to explore new types and patterns of work and so help overcome the problem of meaningless work or unemployment in our society?

What is the nature and purpose of work anyway? How satisfactory are the present modes, choices, and structures of work? In a society from which full employment has probably gone forever, how much responsibility rests upon government and other institutions to redefine work or place less emphasis upon its contribution to society? In what ways do we need an alteration in attitudes to and conditions of work so that jobs can become more suitable and meaningful? Which companies, departments, and organizations are going to provide the models for this? The questions are many, but these are only some of the broader issues that Neil and Sue's dilemma raises.

A Biblical Vision of the People of God

Before exploring in a more systematic way the kinds of issues that ordinary Christians face today, it is important to consider the status and responsibilities the Bible gives to such people. It should not really be necessary to do this. After all, the Reformation in principle overturned the medieval dominance of clerical or monastic over so-called lay or worldly vocations. It reclaimed the biblical vision of the "priesthood of all believers" and of the "secular calling." Unfortunately this reclamation was only partial. As Cyril Eastwood says at the conclusion of his exhaustive two-volume survey of the doctrine of the priesthood of all believers, "No single church has been able to express in its worship, work and witness, the full richness of this doctrine."[2]

Some groups certainly held more truly to the priesthood of all believers than others, especially the Quakers and Moravians, not only in the way they organized their church life but in the significance they attached to their members' calling in the world. Even groups, such as pietists and evangelicals, who stressed lay involvement in church, parachurch, and mission work, still maintained a clerical or elite Christian worker paradigm. So far as their life in the world is concerned, as Mark Gibbs comments, the most resolute believers often have to

> resist the interminable pressures (largely from the clergy who ought to know better) to overemphasize the importance of church structures, and to pretend that it is more Christian to be on a church committee than upon a community school board . . . to be entangled in too much church housekeeping and organization (though, notwithstanding, they often do more than their share in this work) for they know their calling is to be faithful in the structures of the world.[3]

This is why we need to remind ourselves of the biblical vision of the ordinary people of God. While there is much thought expressed on this already in the Old Testament, I will concentrate on the more fully developed New Testament presentation of the believer's contribution in both church and world. It is important to look at both settings, for links between the two were far closer than they tend to be for Christians today.

What signposts does the New Testament set up for understanding the responsibility of ordinary Christians in the church and in the world? Across the whole range of New Testament writings we can discern the following two, at first sign contradictory, declarations, namely, all Christians are "laity" and all Christians are "ministers."

All Christians Are "Laity"

The group described as "the people of God" (Greek, *laos*) refers to the whole body of Jews or Christians (e.g., Titus 2:14). This usage does not exclude, but includes those who play a more visible role in the church. In so speaking it preserves the Old Testament emphasis where, with rare exceptions, the more than 2,000 references to "the people" (Hebrew, *am*) encompasses priests, prophets, the wise, even the king. If the term marks off any group it is those outside the covenant, the Gentiles (Ex. 19:5), though in the New Testament it comprises both Jews and Gentiles (Acts 15:4).

This description of all believers, even leading figures in the church, as "laity," has several correlates:

1. All Christians have a "calling." Basic here is God's call through the Gospel to participate in His work of grace in Christ (1 Cor. 1:9) and all the benefits, such as freedom, peace, hope, eternal life, and glory, that flow from it (Gal. 5:13; Col. 3:15; Eph. 4:4; 1 Tim. 6:12; 2 Peter 1:3). But this also involves a task, that is, "to lead a life worthy of the calling to which you have been called" (Eph. 4:1; cf. 1 Thes. 4:7; 2 Thes. 2:13-14). While this will normally be expressed through any set of circumstances in which people become Christians, that is, the family, work, and social setting they occupied when they first heard the Gospel, it can also be expressed in a new situation or occupation if that opens up (1 Cor. 7:20-21). This call embraces the whole life of believers—it includes their life outside the church as well as their life within it.

We may not find here the more developed sense of vocation that emerges in Luther and even more dynamically in Calvin, where calling is attached to the specific roles people have rather than their basic obligation to live as Christ's people in any context God provides for them. But the root of such an idea is present here as well as in passages where Christians are encouraged to view their present life situations, that is, in family, work, and society (Eph. 5:21–6:18; Col. 3:18–4:17), along with the church, as the primary contexts through which to fulfill their responsibilities.

2. *All Christians are "priests."* Like Israel under the old covenant (Ex. 19:6), Christians are spoken of as a "kingdom of priests," – as a corporate mediator and representative of the reality and grace of God to the nations at large (1 Peter 2:4, 9-10). In reclaiming this conviction, Protestants have tended to spiritualize and individualize it, conceiving each believer as his or her own priest to another believer rather than focusing on the corporate calling of the body of believers vis-a-vis the world around them. While in the Old Testament there was a specialized priesthood within this collective priesthood, as a result of the once-for-all mediatorial work of Christ this specialized priesthood is abolished (Heb. 7–10).

Nevertheless, priestly language continues to be used in the New Testament but now in a metaphorical rather than literal sense. While such language can refer to the apostolic ministry (Rom. 15:16), it is also used of the work of Christians in general. In such passages this language is applied very widely indeed, to their commitment and dedication, sharing in fellowship, and giving of financial aid (Phil. 2:17, 25; Rom. 15:27). The emphasis is not only on what happens in church or among believers, but upon living out the whole of one's life in the light of a developing Christian world view and set of values (Rom. 12:1-2).

3. *All Christians are "saints."* This is one of the New Testament's favorite terms for the people of God (Rom. 1:7; Heb. 13:24; Rev. 8:4). While it is still used of the people of Israel, it is predominantly used of ordinary believers (2 Cor. 1:1). Unlike in later Catholicism and even standard Protestant references to "Saint" Paul, any suggestion that there are different levels of sanctity cuts across the biblical usage. All are "holy" and "set apart" in the sight of God and should embody something of what makes God "holy" and "different" in their own lives.

Generally in the New Testament the term describes a local group of Christians (e.g., 1 Cor. 1:2; 2 Cor. 1:1; Phil. 1:1; Col. 1:2). The word describes a reality that already exists: this is how God views them. It also indicates that it is in their communal, not just individual, life that their distinctiveness should become apparent to those around them. This does not entail withholding themselves from contact with people, even those who reject God's values. On the contrary, it is in the midst of associations with all kinds of people in all the settings of daily life that their uniqueness should be transparent to all (1 Cor. 5:9-10). The common life of Christians should display now a measure of that quality of life already characteristic of heaven.

So then, from one perspective, the New Testament places all believers on the same level. It elevates those who tend to see themselves merely as less important or central to God's work in the church or the world. At the same time the New Testament reminds those who tend to regard themselves as a special group or as having a special status that in these important respects all in God's sight are equal.

All Christians Are "Ministers"

The main cluster of terms used to describe ministry in the New Testament are "serve," "servant," "service" (in Greek, *diakoneo* and cognates). These are the terms from which our word for "ministry" comes. Not surprisingly, apostles and their colleagues are said to be involved in "ministry" as they preach, plan churches, and nurture believers (e.g., Acts 21:19; Col. 4:7). So too are certain people in local congregations who distinguish themselves by the sacrificial nature of their service (1 Cor. 16:15). But the term is also used of Christians generally with respect to exercising their gifts and demonstrating their concern for others (see 1 Cor. 12:5 and Heb. 6:10). As the Swiss theologian Emil Brunner observed:

> All minister . . . nowhere is to be perceived a separation, or even merely a distinction, between those who do not minister, between the active and passive members of the body, between those who give and those who receive. There exists in the ecclesia . . . a universal duty and right of service . . . and at the same time the greatest possible differentiation of functions.[4]

This ministry of Christians to one another by means of God's gifting found concrete expression in their weekly meetings. Not only could all take part collectively, but each was encouraged to share the particular contribution God gave them for the occasion

(1 Cor. 14:26ff). An early Christian meeting was rather like a birthday party to which everyone brought a present, the only difference being that the presents were not for any one person but for everyone. In a sense the whole group had a birthday celebration every Sunday!

This mutual giving and receiving of gifts carried over into their lives with one another outside the meetings as well, not only in their ongoing relationships but their household, workplace, and civic lives (1 Peter 4:8-12). The language of ministry operates outside the church in the world at large. It has to do with Christians fulfilling their everyday obligations in the world and seeking to model a new way of fulfilling those obligations, not just with a concern for evangelism and care directed to others in the world (cf. especially Eph. 5:21-6:18; Col. 3:18-4:6; Titus 2:9-10). Even a secular ruler, acting responsibly, can be described as a "servant" of God (Rom. 13:4).

Within the church, ramifications of this mutual ministry among Christians include the following:

1. All Christians are to engage in caring for one another (Gal. 6:1-2; 1 Cor. 12:25-26). This should automatically be the case between believers on an individual or group basis (1 Thes. 5:14-15), but all should gather together as the whole church to deal with serious problems requiring discipline of another member (1 Cor. 5:4-5).

2. All Christians are to engage in teaching one another (Col. 3:16), so fulfilling the exilic prediction about the mutuality that would mark the new covenant (Jer. 31:31-34). While domineering or authoritarian teaching by women is rejected (1 Tim. 2:12), they can be involved in instructing others if this takes place in an appropriate manner (e.g., Acts 18:26).

3. All Christians are to engage in prophesying to one another (1 Cor. 14:5), so fulfilling the long standing prophetic desire (Num. 11:29) and promise (Joel 2:28-29) which had its firstfruits at Pentecost (cf. Acts 2:17-18). This specifically embraces women, which is interesting in view of Paul's conviction that, after love, prophecy is the greatest contribution one can make to the church.

In view of all this, the New Testament clearly knows no "split-level" distinction between two types of people in the church, ordinary believers and separate leaders, who alone have certain distinctive functions to perform. By virtue of their incorporation into

Christ through baptism and the Spirit, everyone in the church is involved in ministry. This is not to say that the New Testament has an egalitarian understanding of ministry. While everyone from the point of view of status and participation may be placed on the same level, not all operate in the church in identical ways with the same effect. Some distinctions do occur between believers:

1. Believers have different types of gifts. Not all make the same contribution. But each has some gift or mixture of gifts to offer (Rom. 12:4-8; 1 Cor. 12:7-11) and status distinctions are not attached to one or more gifts over the others.

2. Believers have different qualities of functioning. Though all should be involved in instructing and pastoring one another, not all have the ability to do this to the same degree. Some may be therefore described as prophets and teachers (1 Cor. 12:29-31) or as overseers and elders (Phil. 1:1-2; 1 Tim. 3:1). But the distinction between these and the remainder is only a quantitative one. Those in the church who have a more fundamental role to play are still, in our terms, laypeople, marked out from others simply by the extent of their devoted service to the church (1 Cor. 16:15-16; 1 Thes. 5:12-13).

3. Believers have different lengths of stay. Some have a more seminal role to play in the church's life. The most important of these is the church's founding apostle (1 Cor. 4:15 and 3:21-22). Also the founding apostle's colleagues or delegates who come bearing letters, news or have some particular commission to perform (e.g., Timothy and Titus). But all these only reside in a local church temporarily. The apostle begins the work, moves on and returns periodically (cf. Rom. 15:17-24); his co-workers make only intermittent visits (2 Tim. 4:9-12; Titus 3:12); other prophets and teachers are itinerants (Acts 11:27-30). Even Paul works part-time with his hands to make a living, that is, he is sometimes a "tent-maker," not what we tend to call a "full-time worker" (e.g., Acts 18:2-4).

There are also differences in Christian ministry or service outside the church:

1. There are differences in focus. For some their work is mainly within the household (1 Tim. 5:14), for some outside it (Rom. 16:23), for some a mixture of ministry work (Acts 18:3; Rom. 16:3-5).

2. There are differences in status. In some cases people are in

leadership positions, with greater power and freedom (Col. 4:1), in other cases they are subordinates (Col. 3:22-24).

3. There are differences in opportunity. For many there is unlikely to be change in the working environment, yet for some, mobility in this area is possible (1 Cor. 7:21).

The overall impression that emerges in the New Testament is that of the local church as predominantly a people's movement or lay-centered affair, serviced initially and then intermittently by a group of mobile workers almost wholly engaged in preaching, church-planting, and nurturing. It is made up of men, women, and children who as a group take responsibility for the way they church together and develop corporate and individual maturity. Leadership is not vested in one person or a group of persons but in the whole body, though certain people by virtue of their maturity and service, stand out from others and play an important role in the congregation's life. These seminal people do not have a position over the body but within it; they do not so much direct others as "work with" (or alongside) them (2 Cor. 1:24). To quote Orwell, though without the sarcasm he intended, it is a case of "all are equal but some are more equal than others."

In the world of family, work, and civic life outside the church gatherings, it is ordinary believers who play the primary role in bringing a Christian perspective and way of life to bear upon its largely different world view and values. It is clear from the content of Paul's letters that the pressures, concerns, and dilemmas Christians faced in their family, work, and city life, were shared and then prayerfully, scripturally, and prophetically taken up when the church met. The Christian gathering, then, was the crucible through which its members came to discern how to respond with integrity to the dilemmas of everyday life that confronted them. There also appear to be groups which gather in other settings, for example, places where people worked and lived (e.g., Rom. 16:10-11, 14-15).[5]

Recapturing the Vision

In recent times we have seen a recapturing of the vision not only of the role of ordinary Christians but more generally of the connection between faith and daily life. Those involved in this arise in different settings and approach it in different ways. The following three examples involve an ordained Presbyterian who early on felt that his vocation was to be a novelist; a layperson, from the Quaker tradition, who has at various times been a university chaplain, an adult educator, and a member of a residential community; and a Roman Catholic priest who belongs to a religious order. What each of these three writers has in common is their vision of a more integrated understanding of the sacred and the secular, grace and the common life, the supernatural and the everyday.

The first is the highly respected and widely read author Frederick Buechner. A Presbyterian minister, Buechner many years ago realized that his particular calling lay as a writer rather than as pastor in a congregation. Since making that decision he has turned out a steady stream of both fiction and nonfiction. All novels raise the deeper issues in life, especially those relating to God and His ways in the world. His other works address aspects of the relationship between theology and fiction or attempt to do theology in a fresh and very accessible way.

In two of his nonfiction works, *The Sacred Journey* and *Now and Then*, he posits a close connection between autobiography and theology, for the latter is only a more logical, abstract expression of a person's concrete experience of what God has revealed to them. For himself, this experience of God has a decidedly everyday cast about it. As he says of his autobiography:

> More as a novelist than as a theologian, more concretely than abstractly, I determined to try to describe my own life as evocatively and candidly as I could in the hope that such glimmers of theological truth as I believe I had glimpsed in it would shine through my description more or less on their own. It seemed to me then, and it seems to me still, that if God speaks to us at all in this world, if God speaks anywhere, it is into our personal lives that he speaks. Someone we love dies, say. Some unforeseen act of kindness or cruelty touches the heart or makes the blood run cold. We fail a friend, or a friend fails us, and we are appalled at the capacity we all of us have for estranging the very people in our lives we need the most. Or maybe nothing extraordinary happens at all — just one day following another, helter-skelter, in the manner of days. We sleep and dream. We wake. We work. We remember and forget. We have fun and are depressed. And into

the thick of it, or out of the thick of it, at moments of even the most humdrum of our days, God speaks.[6]

This conviction of the link between knowing God and everyday events led Buechner earlier to write a book entitled *The Alphabet of Grace* which focused on a single, ordinary day of his life. In the book, through describing the situations and events that made up the day—waking up, dressing, taking the children to school, working, and coming home again—he sought to suggest something of what he thought God was saying to him.

A second example is provided by Parker Palmer. Unlike, Buechner, his background is in sociology rather than theology. Being a Quaker, he has never sought ordination. In his wonderfully stimulating and original book *The Company of Strangers: Christians and the Renewal of Public Life in America*, Palmer reveals aspects of his own pilgrimage. His journey has led him to become a member of a residential community. He has also had a close association with, indeed helped initiate, an institute and center concerned to relate Christianity and life in the world. He has also been closely involved with the development of theological education for the wider Christian public.

Although, as the title of his provocative book suggests, he is dealing more with the public arena of life, he does not define this in the narrow terms of the political dimension. As Palmer defines it, this arena covers more of what we might term "all the business of life" than the title of his book appears to suggest. For example, he identifies some of the places where public life comes to regular expression:

The most likely place is the public street where strangers in pursuit of private interests meet each other . . . city parks, squares, sidewalk cafes, museums, and galleries are also settings for the public life. . . . Rallies, forums, hearings and debates (including those conducted by means of the public media) are settings in which the public interacts and becomes aware of itself. . . . The neighborhood is another important setting for public life. Voluntary associations are also settings in which strangers come together and receive training. . . . So the settings in which public life happens are many and diverse.[7]

Here, then, is another's story and approach to some of the same issues, forcefully and imaginatively argued, with wide-ranging implications for Christian thought and behavior.

Since writing that book Parker Palmer has completed another that grew out of his own struggle and ultimately failure to live in a community that tried to adapt monastic practices to ordinary life. In this book on *The Active Life* he plants spirituality firmly within the texture of daily situations and responsibilities. Instead of emphasizing, as many approaches to spirituality do, withdrawal from the world and undistracted contemplation, he explores the possibility of an active and down-to-earth spirituality that possesses a contemplative dimension.[8]

A third example of someone wrestling with the relevance of everyday experience for our understanding of God and obedience to him is Charles Cummings. His situation is very different from that of either Buechner or Palmer. In one sense he seems to be removed from many of the demands of life that most people face, for Cummings belongs to a Roman Catholic order, one that operates according to quite stringent disciplines. But we have learned from Thomas Merton that the contemplative life can sometimes put a person into closer contact with certain realities of everyday life than a more activist approach, precisely because the contemplative really does engage with those realities rather than simply hurrying through them.

This is the case with Charles Cummings who has undertaken advanced study in the area of spiritual formation and has committed himself to exploring contemporary modes of spiritual deepening for the benefit of ordinary Christians. In particular, drawing on a quarter of a century of reflection on ordinary aspects of life, he seeks to show others how much relating to and following God is interwoven with the texture of the simplest daily activities:

We may live in extraordinary times, but most of us spend the greater part of our existence doing quite ordinary things. Our simple, everyday experiences can, however, put us in touch with the deepest mystery of life. . . . Unfortunately the sameness and repetition of everyday activities can numb our awareness to the power. We get nothing out of the ordinary, and so conclude that nothing of value is there. Instead we seek extraordinary experiences and the special techniques that might induce such states. We put religious experience too easily into the category of the unusual, and never expect to find God in the usual things we do. The rich, spiritual dimension of our ordinary activities is thus lost to us.[9]

In his book *The Mystery of the Ordinary*, Cummings looks at such routine activities as hearing, seeing, walking, resting, standing, and eating, suggesting ways in which God is present in or can be served through them. Whereas Buechner concentrates on the relevance of the commonplace for one's life journey or vocation, and Palmer for our public life and responsibilities, Cummings attends more to its significance for our understanding of God and the transformation of our character.

So, then, just as there are various stories to be told from the side of ordinary Christians about the everyday issues that confront them, so there are other stories from the side of those who are seeking to bring theological insight to play in *redeeming the routines* of everyday life.[10]

How This Book Came About

I have made it clear, I hope, that this book is not just an intellectual exercise, but has arisen out of increasing practical involvement in the issues it raises. It is not enough to think about the problem and then throw out a few untried suggestions. We have too much of this already in the contemporary church, and it has not overcome much of our present irrelevance. I realize that in some Christian circles there is too much doing and not enough thinking. That creates its own set of problems, many of which distract us from the real work God wishes us to do. Here I wish merely to emphasize the need for a closer and reciprocal connection between study and activity, thinking and doing, writing and experimenting.

This book did not only arise out of practical involvement in the area under discussion. It was stimulated by meeting with people from a number of Christian organizations in my own city who are seeking to help Christians relate their faith to their everyday lives. For me it has been essentially a practical exercise.

If you are a professional theologian or Christian educator, I have sought to address your concerns at points in the book. But throughout I have had a broader audience in view. If you are wanting to integrate your beliefs with your everyday life in a thoughtful way, then I am writing for you as well. I even have an eye on those of you who may not be convinced about Christianity, but have become aware that there is a spiritual dimension to life and that this should have a practical bearing upon your life.

But right at this point I have a difficulty. Such is the gap between theologians on the one hand and thoughtful Christians on the other, let alone those who are not yet persuaded to become Christians, that it is hard to know how to speak to all three groups at the same time. For example, a friend who has been manager of several Christian and general bookstores told me that the appearance of the word *theology* in the title of this book would be "the kiss of death" so far as marketing it to the general public. But for a professional theologian or theological student, it is the very presence of "theology" in the title that is likely to attract attention. The word *theology* is just one example of the problem of writing for a diverse audience. On the whole these groups have different starting points, use different language, and argue in different ways.

But I have taken the plunge, hoping there will be readers from all three groups at the other end of the page. I take heart from the comments of two writers who have attempted to bridge this gap. The successful German theological communicator, Helmut Thielicke, said that when he wished to draw people into his church in Hamburg who were not there at present, he prepared addresses for and spoke to them even though he knew they would not initially turn up. Only so would they actually begin to come! C.S. Lewis also once observed that it was far easier to write for a specialized audience than for a broader one, but that there was a greater need to write for the latter. In so doing both groups would actually be catered to.

So then I have tried to keep technical terms and theological jargon to a minimum. Yet I have not been afraid to use such language where it gives more precision to the argument or is a convenient form of shorthand. On the whole I have avoided discussion of pedantic theological points since these will be unfamiliar to many and would not warrant the extra space needed to explain them satisfactorily. But for those interested, the appendix contains a discussion of some representative works and movements. Here and there, I have also provided endnotes that point the way to helpful resources.

I would not want you to begin this book with false expectations. If you come to it uncertain about the extent to which there is a divorce between Christian thinking and all the routines of life, but open to find out to what extent this exists, you will find ample to help you work this out. I have gone into some detail about the size and character of this gap and have discussed why it exists and who is chiefly to blame. You will also find a strong challenge to you to do something to overcome it. But I have not attempted to present a complete set of arguments or testimonies to undergird my case.

If, on the other hand, you are only too well aware of the gap between your faith and your everyday life, and desperately want to close that gap, this book will not do it all for you. This is not because I have failed to wrestle enough with the problem, nor because I have failed to give practical suggestions as to what you might do. It does not close the gap because you are the only one who can do so. I have outlined the range of issues which require attention and identified the obstacles which must be overcome. I will point you to ways in which you could begin to bridge the gap and to resources which will help you along the way. More than that I cannot do. Otherwise I take too much of the privilege and responsibility for what needs to be done out of your hands.

Finally, I also want to allay in advance fears that some people express about too great a concentration upon everyday aspects of life, feeling perhaps that it diverts attention from the main task of commending the Gospel to the people around us. One of the continuing threads throughout this book is the relationship between practical obedience and evangelistic concern. In one sense, the book is an extended commentary on the biblical injunction not to be conformed to this world but to present our whole selves as living sacrifices to God (Rom. 12:1-2). In another sense, it fleshes out the notion that verbal presentation of the Gospel is inadequate unless it is framed within what is commonly referred to as lifestyle evangelism. In addition, the book suggests that it is disturbing that we provoke so little interest in and so few questions about the Gospel.

It also suggests that the reason why much preaching and teaching fails to strike home is because it does not begin from or connect up with real-life situations and dilemmas that everyone faces. As Jacques Ellul says:

I know very well that people will say: "Isn't simple preaching enough?" In reality the so-called confidence in the "efficacy of the word of God" betrays a lack of charity towards men and an indifference to their actual situation; to some extent it is a "spirituality" which is not in accordance with the mind of Christ.

The Bible always shows us God laying hold of man in his practical situation; in the setting of his life, enabling him to act with the means of his own time, in the midst of the problems of his own day. But to want to copy the methods of Irenaeus or of Calvin means that we are both mistaken and unfaithful . . . our own day presents very complicated problems; our organization is more complex than that of past centuries; and the same is true of questions which challenge the Christian faith and conscience . . . in the heart of this conflict, the word can be proclaimed but nowhere else.

When we have really understood the actual plight of our contemporaries, when we have heard their cry of anguish, when we have understood why they won't have anything to do with our "disembodied Gospel," when we have shared their sufferings, both physical and spiritual, in their despair and desolation, when we have become one with the people of our own nation . . . as Moses and Jeremiah were one with their own people, as Jesus identified himself with the wandering crowds, "sheep without a shepherd," *then* we shall be able to proclaim the word of God—but not till then![11]

Unless we can do something about the pressures people live with today, they will be more closed to the Gospel than they need be. In all these and other ways, as you will see, there is a close link between the concerns of this book and the fundamental place of evangelism.

Questions for Reflection:

1. Do you think there can be a theology of sleep? If so, what is yours?
2. How should we divide our responsibilities between work, church, and home?
3. What part should sports play in our lives? What is good and bad about the role of sports in our culture?

4. If you were in Jan's shoes (pages 21-23), what would your vocation be?

5. How can city life serve our life goals better than it does at the moment?

6. What changes do you think there should be in work patterns?

Two
The Credibility Gap

I need to say a word about some of the terms that I am using continually throughout this book. In discussing the gap that so often exists between our basic system of beliefs and the general routines of life, I have suggested the need for what I have called a "theology of everyday life." In order to avoid possible confusion, I wish to look at the way in which these words are being used.

The Meaning of the Key Terms

1. What Exactly Is Theology?

During a visit some months ago, a pastor from one of the churches in my home city commented, "Of course mine is a fairly typical congregation — not interested in theology or anything like that." He was right. Most Christians do not view theology in a positive light. The word suggests something rather esoteric. It has an otherworldly ring about it. As for people outside the church, long ago I found that describing myself as a theologian was usually the end of the conversation. Either they changed the topic or moved on hurriedly to someone else in the room. Someone who introduced himself as an astrologist would probably get a better hearing.

What about people who have no trouble with the word? What does the word *theology* mean to them? Normally it refers to the activity of exploring and organizing Christian beliefs in a systemat-

4 3

ic way. This is carried out by a group of specialists who have high academic qualifications in the area. You normally find theology in learned books and articles, in seminaries and religious studies departments, in professional conferences and seminars. But this usage is too narrow. Theology is—or ought to be—a much wider enterprise. In fact, part of the problem the average person has with theology stems from the fact that it seems to exist in a specialized world of its own.

But how broadly should we understand it? Occasionally you will hear someone suggest that it refers to any attitude toward Christianity, however rudimentary or unsystematic that may be. Just as people talk about everyone having some "philosophy of life," so all Christians necessarily have a theology of some kind. This theology is made up of knowledge derived from sermons or conferences, personal reading and study groups, tapes or articles.

Now undoubtedly everyone does have views about life as well as values they live by. Christians also have some notion of what they believe in and how they should conduct themselves. But it is not very helpful to describe the first as a philosophy and the second as a theology of life unless a person reflects on and organizes their beliefs in some degree. The seeds of a theology may exist prior to someone doing this, but nothing more.

In order for you to have a theology, therefore, you must give some thought to what you believe and develop some coherence in your understanding. Not everyone does this, not even those who engage in personal or group Bible study. Such study may be so devotional in orientation that very little genuine thinking takes place. Or thinking may take place within so rigid a doctrinal framework that people do not have the freedom to develop their own understanding of God and His ways. I do not mean that devotional concern and strong convictions are incompatible with theology. It is just that in themselves these are not enough to constitute it. Nor am I saying that only those with formal education can have a theology. All you need is a willingness to think about truth and organize your conclusions. This is by no means confined to nor is it guaranteed by possession of an academic degree.

What then about learning that takes place through Christian education programs in local churches, parachurch groups, or church colleges? Here we are on firmer ground. These tend to invite more serious discussion and to be more highly focused.

Occasionally they lack sufficient depth to take people very far. Sometimes they are too piecemeal in their approach. But at their best, they provide a pathway to a maturer and more ordered understanding. For that reason it is a pity that such programs tend to be described as Christian rather than theological education. This is somewhat of a put-down, for it reserves theological education for those who go to "academic" Christian institutions or read "serious" religious books.

Between this type of theological learning and the most sophisticated postgraduate forms, there are many intermediate levels, as there are between so-called Christian education programs and personal or group Bible study. Also it would be a mistake to think that theology only had to do with the Bible or with lectures and libraries. Theology comes from the wisdom you distill through quiet and disciplined reflection on the world God has created or upon the nature of life in general. The quest for understanding of the experience of God in your life and the desire to integrate this with other things you have learned also leads to theological understanding. So too does conversation with God, where this involves regular and sustained meditation on who He is and what He asks. In fact, any of these can be more genuinely theological than certain kinds of academic study of theology. Though the latter may focus on some aspect of Christianity in a concentrated way, the thinking that goes on may take place at a purely historical or philosophical level. Even study of the Bible or of systematic theology in such a setting can be a purely intellectual exercise. There is little vital personal involvement through the subject matter with God Himself and little concern to practice what is understood.

When I use the word *theology* in this book, then, I am referring to *any endeavor on the part of Christians to think through and set in order their beliefs, with the intention of drawing closer to God and reflecting more of His character in their lives.* Where I have the more sophisticated type of theology in mind, I shall qualify the term by words such as "professional" or "academic." In doing this I am not, by means of an inverse snobbery, dismissing its value. High-level theology has its place. It has a real contribution to make to understanding everyday life from a Christian point of view. But this requires changes in the prevailing attitudes and models which govern so much of it. As for theology in the broader sense, sometimes I have used synonyms such as "thinking Christianly," "de-

veloping a Christian perspective," "gaining a Christian understanding," and "redeeming routine aspects of life." I have done
this to avoid overuse of the word *theology,* especially since it may
still be a barrier to some of you reading this book.

2. What Makes Up Everyday Life?

The term *everyday life* seems clear enough but it is not as obvious
in meaning as it appears. This is a shorthand way of talking about
what the title of this book refers to as the "routine" dimension of
life. In general by *everyday life* I mean the regular situations we
find ourselves in throughout the day or week, the ongoing responsibilities we have or activities we engage in, the issues that regularly claim our attention, the most insistent pressures that we feel,
the things that we commonly think and talk about, the desires,
values, and beliefs that most shape our lives. I shall spell these out
in more detail in the following chapter.

Obviously not everyone would describe what makes up their
everyday life in identical terms: it is a complex and many-sided
affair, varying according to factors such as gender, class, and nationality. As a result they look at life differently, feel differently
about even the same things, and respond differently to similar
circumstances. For example, men and women do not always approach people, issues, or situations in the same way. In a similar
fashion, the socioeconomic level at which you live tends to affect
the way you view the world and react to it. This is more noticeable
when we consider ethnic differences where a great deal of humor
and tragedy has resulted from the clashing perceptions of people
who belong to different ethnic groups. Other differences such as
how old we are, where we live, how much formal education we
have had, and whether we are handicapped or not, alter our understanding and experience of everyday life.

So when I use the phrase *everyday life* I am talking about a
multiple reality and to do it justice we need a variety of attempts
to think Christianly or theologize about it. These would have different groups as their focus and be written in a different style, for
the style needs to match the audience for which it is intended.
While there would be a number of common threads between classes, each would also have distinctive elements. I am writing as a
male, middle-class Anglo-Saxon. Though I have made a genuine
attempt to think beyond this and enter into others' situations, my

choice of concerns and the way I approach them will be partly affected by who, where, and what I am.

How far have the issues of everyday life been addressed by professional theologians? Although various schools of thought have turned in its direction during the last thirty years, they have only explored some of its territory.

During the sixties two theological movements emerged that were distinct but in part overlapped in content, namely *secular* and *political theology*. Central to the first was the belief that religion as it had been traditionally defined was no longer an option for modern people. The Christian message therefore needed secular translation into nonreligious, more everyday, terms. This resulted in a shift of interest from theology to ethics and from belief to behavior. Political theology did not begin from the same premise. It arose from the conviction that Christian thought had underemphasized the influence of social and political structures. It was necessary to bring these into sharper relief and to spell out more clearly the inherent political dimension of Gospel.[1]

So then, both these theological movements attempted to draw our attention to the importance of what *we* could do about these concerns. Much emphasis was laid on the need for Christians to come to grips more positively with the secular nature of modern society and to become politically involved in making it a more human place in which to live. These movements generally looked at the world through a large telescope, identifying trends that we needed to be aware of or reminding us of measures we could take to influence our society. This was helpful, even if they did overplay the extent to which our society is really secular and the amount that can be achieved through the political process. But neither of these approaches brought into focus our day-to-day concerns and activities in a close-up way.

Over the last decade and a half there has also been considerable interest in developing a *contextual and local theology*. Too often in the past professional theologians have ignored the concrete situation in which they worked and the particular society of which they were a part. For example, I cannot remember any serious attention being given in my theological education to the fact that both myself and the people around me had been shaped by the particular history and geography associated with being Australian. It was as if place or nationality had no bearing whatever on what people were like or on how I might bring the Gospel to them. But now some Christian thinkers have begun to identify what is distinctive about life in our own countries and to discuss how living in them affects us.

Part of the solution is to develop an *indigenous theology*, that is, not just translating or adapting theology to its context but doing theology itself in an indigenous or culturally appropriate way. This might entail shifts of emphasis not just in content but also in the way theology itself is understood and undertaken. Such an approach is more complex than it first looks. Any one context may contain a variety of social, economic, racial, and religious groups. In some measure theology needs to be incarnated in each of these settings. A contextual or local theology certainly produces materials relevant to a theology of everyday life, especially at the level of a people's basic orientation, values, and rites. But it does not accord significance to the full range of ordinary situations and activities that make up so much of our lives.[2]

In recent years we have seen a renewed interest in *personal and social ethics*. Some of the work that has been done in this area is fairly theoretical. Some of it has taken up personal moral dilemmas that many people, including Christians, face, such as divorce and remarriage. A number of issues that concern these writers—abortion or euthanasia, for example—are faced less frequently by individuals but have become increasingly important, and divisive, issues in our society. Many of the broader social dilemmas these writers address—unemployment or the nuclear threat, for instance—do impinge upon our lives in a real way and form the context in which we live.

One of the key contributions of this new approach to ethics has been the stress upon the importance of character in decision-making and the role of story or narrative in personal life and the biblical tradition. Yet these writers do not always give us much guidance as to what we can do at a practical level about these and other problems. This guidance has been given most fully in the area of lifestyle, though it is not always professional theologians who have the most helpful things to say. In any case, life is more than a series of moral ethical issues, for not all the daily situations we negotiate and priorities we have to order primarily raise moral choices.[3]

There has also been renewed interest in *pastoral* and *practical theology. Pastoral theology* deals with such matters as rites of passage and different life stages as well as some of the dilemmas of personal and family life. The theological appraisal of these enters the sphere of everyday life in a significant way, but only touches certain aspects of it. Moreover it does so only through the eyes of the ordained person, who remains central to the whole enterprise. Even though de facto the number of part- or full-time lay pastors is increasing, or the responsibilities of deacons and sometimes elders are moving in a more pastoral direction, where such people develop pastoral theological concerns this is still within the limits of a professional definition of ministry.

In the past, *practical theology* has concentrated on various dimensions of ordained ministry such as preaching, liturgy, religious education, and church management. Now it is being widened to include the vocation of all Christians, in the world as well as in the church. So viewed, this also overlaps with a theology of everyday life, but to date the emphasis has fallen upon an expanded approach to clerical training, or upon a primary concern with social justice and global issues. In both, the church remains central as a context for theologizing, not the home, workplace, or community which are often more relevant.[4]

The two theological movements which have a decided everyday life dimension are *lay theology* and the grass roots form of *liberation theology*. *Lay theology* is primarily a First World phenomenon and some of its chief landmarks over the last generation are surveyed in Appendix A. At present it is a growing phenomenon, especially in the areas of relating faith to work, spirituality, and daily life. After a decidedly academic start, a second, more grassroots, form of *liberation theology* began to develop. This took place when several of its key spokespeople associated themselves with basic Christian communities on the edge of large cities and started dealing with the daily concerns of the people. Here too there has been a growing concern with the spirituality as well as a theology of everyday life.

In many respects this book represents an extension of what these two movements offer. I prefer to speak of an "everyday" rather than "lay" or "liberation" theology. In the first instance this is because it is precisely the division between clerical and lay that needs to be overcome. While there is a specific contribution to be made by certain people in the church more than others, the theology in which they "live, move, and have their being," is not essentially a different kind of theology to that which should inform all believers. The word "liberation," I believe, is too narrow, even in more oppressed Third World contexts, not only because liberation in the full sense is not always possible, but because our Christian responsibility involves leavening and transforming social structures, not always liberating them in the fullest sense.[5]

The Gap between Belief and Daily Life

In the remainder of this chapter I would like to formulate ten theses. These have their basis in the experiences of a wide range of people who have corroborated or extended my own conclusions about the relationship between belief and the routines of everyday life. Some of these people I have met, corresponded with, and engaged in discussion. Others are only known to me through their writings. In each of the statements that follow I have drawn on the experience of one of these people. The first five of these theses will explore the gap many of us perceive between our faith and our everyday lives. All I am doing in this section is building on what is common knowledge to those seeking to develop an integrated Christian life. The final five of these will examine the gap that exists between theology as it is written and taught today and everyday life. Less has been written about this and the gap is far wider than most imagine.

1. Few of us apply or know how to apply our belief to our work, or lack of work.
In the mid-1970s a book appeared entitled *Christianity and Real Life*, written by the sales manager for a major overseas steel corporation. I came across the book a couple of years later and it struck deep chords in my own mind. For here was a thinking Christian, speaking from the heart of the modern workplace, who wrote in an anguished way about the credibility gap he felt in his own life. In the preface to the book, William Diehl wrote:

> This book is about two gaps. The first gap is the one which is present in my life and in the lives of thousands of dedicated laypeople. It is the gap between our Sunday faith and our weekday world.

The second gap is the one ... between what the church
proclaims as the role of Christian laypersons in the world and
what the church actually does to support that role.
The two gaps are closely interrelated.[6]

I will say more about the second of these gaps later. Here I simply
wish to underline the distance Diehl was aware of between his
religious beliefs and his responsibilities at work.

Many other Christians are also conscious of this gap. Some of
you may be troubled by the pressures you are under at work.
Others may feel frustrated because of the kind of work you have to
do. Or you may be concerned about the quality of the decisions
you have to make, the values of the place you work for, the
structures within which you carry out your job, or the goals of the
institution in which you serve. In his book Diehl only concerns
himself with work of this kind, that is with paid employment. But
there are many other kinds of work and they also raise questions
for those undertaking them.

Work may take the form of housework, study, voluntary help, or
vocational training, as well as paid employment. Work needs to be
understood more widely than it is in most discussions of a "lay
theology." Such discussions leave too many people out of account
and, incidentally, give these the impression that they do not make
much of a contribution. Interpreting it in its broadest sense, work
occupies more of our time than any other activity. This gives it a
special significance in our lives.

Despite a gradual lowering of statutory and actual working
hours, certain groups in our society are now working longer than
ever before. It's now very common to find such people regularly
bringing home work in the evenings or over the weekend. Despite
the proliferation of labor-saving devices, the increased size of
homes and yards today and the increased expectations about clean-
liness and presentation have resulted in little reduction in the
number of hours spent on domestic work. There has also been a
fairly steady rise in the amount of time young people give to their
education or training. In addition to this time factor, many women
are confused about the status and value of the work involved in
raising a family and looking after a home. Some students are uncertain about the vocational or personal value of the studies they
have to undertake. And in the official workforce itself, more and

more people appear to be experiencing a mid-life crisis.

We also have the problem of long-term or endemic unemployment to worry about. Jobs are now much harder to get. Educational qualifications do not guarantee employment anymore, though they certainly help. If you are older you have more chance, but middle-aged people as well as the young are now victims of our economic misfortunes. Many more of you will be out of work in the future or only be able to get part-time jobs. Our economy is on a continuing downturn and there is no reversal in sight.

This situation is raising broader questions about the nature, significance, and character of work. But these are already real issues for some people. Some of you are facing a threat to your job, if not right now then at some point down the road. Some of you have a job, but it is not the one you trained for or would prefer to have. You may even have formal theological qualifications or be a pastor and experience this. Some of you are wondering whether you should now head in a new direction. If you are in any of these situations, how well have you been able to make sense Christianly of what is happening to you?

2. We make only minimal connections between our faith and our spare time activities.
What people do in their spare time varies in importance from one person to the next. For some it is secondary to their main concerns. For others it is central to their lives. Recently, I was talking to a friend about this. In the course of our conversation he told me about a young married woman who attended his church. This woman had discovered within herself a deep interest in art. She had begun to attend classes to learn more about it and to develop her creative skills. While she gave the major part of her time to bringing up her small family, whatever time was left over she devoted to her newfound interest. This interest had helped overcome her feeling of simply being an extension of her husband and children. It had enriched and given added meaning to her life.

It was bringing out gifts within her that she never knew she possessed. Yet she was having difficulty integrating it with her Christianity. She found it hard to talk to people about what she was doing, for no one seemed to be able to enter into it. She knew of no other models for bringing together these two aspects of her life. The world of other Christians and the world of her art interests never seemed to meet. So much so that she admitted to my friend that when she went to church on Sundays "so narrow is the scope of what I can talk about and what happens that I feel I have to leave half of myself behind at home."

Not everyone would place as much importance on their leisure time activities as this young woman. But that does not mean that those activities are insignificant either for ourselves or for God. Of course some people do not have much spare time anyway. Sometimes economic necessities in low income families force one or more members of a family to take on two jobs to "moonlight." The long distances some people have to travel to get to work places pressures upon their time and occasionally even breaks a family up. The person bringing up children in a single-parent family faces extra demands that sometimes leaves one little time for leisure. Women with a number of young children often find little rest from early morning to well on in the evening. Young couples trying to buy a home are both under pressure these days to work for some years in order to save a down payment. In such cases the problem is how to create sufficient leisure time for relaxation and refreshment. However, while many of us have less free time than we realize — why else would we be complaining so much about how little time we have? — on average most of us can devote up to 10 precent of our time to freely chosen activities. We use this time in different ways, and many are finding it difficult to judge how to use this time in the most fitting way.

Part of the problem is due to the feeling that these days many leisure time activities involve harder work than our weekday jobs. Some believe it is better to keep up the addictive pace of work in their spare time rather than face the painful withdrawal symptoms they would have if they really relaxed. On the other hand, some are also becoming aware that it is easy to reduce leisure pursuits merely into an escape from work or compensation for work. How can we honor the spirit of the fourth commandment (Ex. 20:8-11) in our kind of society and turn our leisure time activities into the fulfillment of our work, an end in themselves, with their own distinctive rhythms and rewards?

But many of us feel guilty about taking time off to do "nothing much" when we have free time, even though we know it is one of the things God has commanded. Generally we find it difficult to establish a balance between work and leisure. We are also unsure how to proportion leisure and church-related activities. Yet apart from hesitating to play in games on Sundays and having a sense that sports is all about fair play, few of us have any idea about how we might develop a Christian perspective on our leisure time.

3. We have little sense of a Christian approach to regular activities. Every so often I come across people who feel bound and frustrated by their circumstances. This can happen both to those whose main focus of work is in the home and to those who have found work outside it. As one homemaker said, "Sometimes I feel that I'm just stuck in the house, tied to the kitchen sink and washing machine. All I seem to do is clean up after the kids—just one thing after another. I spend half the evening catching up on chores I haven't been able to do during the day. I hardly ever open a book or if I do I get only part of the way through it. Some days I get so frustrated that I could bang my head against the wall until I drop." Not all people who work at home feel this way; some find deep satisfaction in such work and manage to strike a balance between it and other activities.

I have heard others talk in a similar way about their frustrations in the work force. Many people—both men and women—feel dissatisfied with the jobs they do. This is frequently the case in much large-scale factory work, in the pedestrian character of many low-level office jobs, or in certain positions held down in stores and supermarkets. A particularly severe instance of this is the underpaid, high-pressured work that goes on in many textile industries, much of which exploits the services of migrant women who find it difficult to get other employment. But not all our routine situations are this extreme or as depressing as this example. If you work at home you probably find certain things that you do or certain times of the day more congenial than others. If you work outside it, there are many things you do before you start work at 9:00 in the morning, during your lunch hour, and after 5:00 in the evening which have to be done but are not necessarily frustrating. In both cases there are also activities you engage in on weekends and on holidays, apart from leisure pursuits.

These are not all or always draining, though sometimes they can become rather monotonous. Most of our time goes simply on personal maintenance. Sleeping, as we noted earlier, takes up nearly a third of our time, while washing, dressing, grooming, and eating occupy another 10 percent of our time over our total life span. If you are employed, when you add personal maintenance to your domestic chores, this amounts to approximately the same amount of time you spend at work—competing for almost another third of your time. If you are mainly a homemaker, you spend only marginally less time on these two activities than those in paid employment. Then there is the time spent in shopping, chauffering children, running errands, and attending meetings: about 5 percent of our time overall is spent on traveling.

Quite apart from these activities and the daily round of domestic chores, both work and leisure can contain a routine element. For example, if you are employed, much of what you do in the early stages of your career can be fairly monotonous. So too if you are still at school or attending a college or university. The apparent meaninglessness of so much routine activity lies at the root of many personal problems. Yet, apart from memories of the example of Brother Lawrence at the kitchen sink and admonitions about learning to be content in every situation, how are we able to tie in our routine activities with the obligation to place the kingdom of God first in our lives? Some Christians are deeply aware of this gap. But since they cannot remain too long in it, frequently they look for an escape into some "Christian" work that has more apparent meaning or they resign themselves to "wasting" much of their time each day on humdrum matters. Yet others will not settle for this and persist in seeking a better alternative.

4. *Our everyday attitudes are partly shaped by the dominant values of our society.*
A couple of years ago a multi-denominational survey was carried out to discover the dominant values of American people. The results of this survey by the Search Institute in Minneapolis are disturbing. Its investigation of the everyday attitudes and standards of churchgoers concluded that there were only minimal differences between them and those not active in church. In this area even the practice of sectarian Christian groups was not all that dissimilar to the population at large. They do exhibit a different attitude on some personal and social moral issues, but this is less noticeable in some of their basic goals and values.[7]

Comparisons with other Western countries suggest that the attitudes and priorities of Christians within them are not dissimilar.

The same social forces, norms, and pressures affect us all and many of these operate in hidden and pervasive ways which are difficult to detect and resist. Many Christians do have a strong sense of their fundamental beliefs and standards, but find it difficult to know exactly how these apply to the varied and complex situations that confront them. Most of us have an innate suspicion of materialistic attitudes, of becoming worldly, and of a relaxed approach to morals. But it is hard to remain unaffected by the acquisitive impulse, to discern the subtle forms which worldliness takes, or to know how to deal with gray rather than black-and-white moral situations.

This is why a gap so often opens up between the private profession of faith and its public performance. This does not necessarily make Christians hypocrites in the sense in which that term is used today, for mostly they want to avoid living in a way that is self-contradictory. But it does make Christians hypocrites in the biblical sense of the word. That is, they say one thing but without realizing it do another. Christians are unaware how much they are influenced by the basic assumptions, such as individualism, on which our society rests, or by its ideological attitudes, such as increasingly having a consumer attitude, even toward the church and God.

Some Christians sense this and are trying to do something about it. They want to identify their underlying beliefs and values and find out how consonant they are with Christ's teaching. They want to apply that teaching to the tangled web of pressures, aspirations, dilemmas, concerns, and situations that daily come their way. But, as they are discovering, this is not easy. Quite apart from anything else, there is so much to think through, decide on, and do something about. What matters should have priority and what do they do about those matters that for the time being they have to leave to one side? Even with the help of others it is a slow, often confusing, and sometimes painful process.

5. *Many of our spiritual difficulties stem from the daily pressures we experience.*

Some time ago I received an interesting letter from a regional denominational head. This came as a response to a short article I had written on how few Christians bought or read books of a religious nature. In the article I talked about the poor quality and especially the unreality of so much Christian literature. Taking up what I said about the irrelevance of so much Christian literature to the concerns of the average Christian, the Bishop asked how much research had been done on the day-to-day problems that the majority of Christians face. He had begun to see the need for this, he said, as the result of a recent experience in his Diocese:

Recently I conducted a mission in a nearby country town. Before I conducted the mission I asked each member of the Parish Council to answer a question, and the question I put was, "What is it in your Christian experience that most deters you from Christian belief or Christian behavior? In other words, what is the single element that makes it most difficult for you to believe and behave in a Christian manner?" I asked each member of the Parish Council to do that exercise privately and not to confer with other members of the Council. I then collected the results and was astonished to find that more than half of them said that the one thing that most prevented them from believing and behaving as a Christian was the nature of society itself. The most common element that set up this hurdle was the pressures they found in society. I had anticipated getting answers like how difficult it was to understand or read the Bible, or how unreal it seemed to be saying prayers, or other answers of a semireligious nature. For the purposes of that Mission I changed the whole teaching and first of all tried to describe modern society and then to suggest some Christian answers.

Of course, some people—both within the church and outside it— do have genuine intellectual or moral problems with Christianity. However, most do not, even when they cast their questions in the form of intellectual and moral objections. Some people's difficulties with Christianity do arise from a lack of biblical knowledge or an inadequate devotional life. But often it is external factors which make it hard for people to make time to read the Bible and pray, not some inner weakness. Even those who manage to overcome these difficulties sometimes find it hard to relate what they believe and what they read in the Bible to their daily responsibilities. When they go to church they may find it difficult to relate the sermon and prayers to what they are involved in during the remainder of the week.

This gap between religious convictions and ordinary activities is due to a number of factors. For example, if in the office or factory where people work they are only able to refer to God occasionally, it is easy for them to begin thinking and talking less about God in general. As well, since they need a pragmatic outlook to function well on the job, this slowly begins to affect the way they approach non-work areas of life, even what goes on in their church or spiritual life. Alternatively, a deadening or impersonal job can in the long term have a dulling effect upon people's personality, outlook, and relations in general, carrying over into the spiritual dimension as well. This is part of the reason why so many blue collar workers have been alienated in the past from Christianity and are still less attracted to it today.

Busyness and the need to work late also start to impinge upon the quality of their relating to God and others. These are some of the reasons why so many Christians are reticent about their faith at work. (It also explains why some become hyper-spiritual, compensating for the lack of religious dimension in their work by taking a charismatic overdose elsewhere.) Ministers frequently trace this gap to a lack of singlemindedness toward Christ. But it is not yielding to obvious temptations from the world that is always the problem. It is the discordance people feel between the world they inhabit most of the week and the world of churchgoing and religious practices.

6. Our everyday concerns receive little attention in the church.
A number of years ago my wife and I were leading a mission in a mainline church in the South Island of New Zealand. This ran over three weeks and included a mixture of sermons, addresses, seminars, dialogues, and conversations. We decided to focus the mission on the theme "Getting in Touch," looking in turn at how to establish contact with oneself, others, and God. The mission began with an opening service at which I preached on the way busyness resulted in our losing touch with all of these. After the service I was approached by a middle-aged businessman who said that he did not go to church very often. "When my wife reminded me that the mission was starting this morning," he said, "I tossed up whether I would bother coming or not. I thought to myself 'You'll only have to sit through another sermon, so what's the point?' I almost didn't come. But when you spoke, I didn't hear a sermon at

all. Instead I heard someone talking about what was actually going on in my own life."

His reaction is most revealing. For him, and I suspect many others, a sermon by definition did not bear any relation to everyday life. It was something otherworldly, in the worst rather than best sense of the term. Helmut Thielicke writes about this problem in his book, *The Trouble with the Church:*

> The real crisis in preaching under which we are suffering [is] a modern variant of Docetism . . . when a sermon does not "hit home," the reason need by no means lie in the fact that it contained no examples from life nor that it was too theoretical . . . it may lie in the fact that the preacher is speaking on the basis of a Docetic view of human beings and that the person of whom he is speaking and whom he is addressing does not appear in the sermon at all. Then the very hearers who are troubled by real situational problems feel that they have been bypassed. And perhaps the only ones who listen are those who are largely removed from the worldly situation.[8]

This is why, as Thielicke goes on to mention, the majority of Christians making a vital contribution today are not attending such services of worship. But what is true of sermons is true of church activities in general. To quote William Diehl again:

> In the almost thirty years of my professional career, my church has never once suggested that there be any type of accounting of my on-the-job ministry to others. My church has never once offered to improve those skills which could make me a better minister, nor has it ever asked if I needed any kind of support in what I was doing. There has never been an inquiry into the types of ethical decisions I must face, or whether I seek to communicate the faith to my coworkers. I have never been in a congregation where there was any type of public affirmation of a ministry in my career. In short, I must conclude that my church really doesn't have the least interest whether or how I minister in my daily work.[9]

Most Bible studies are of little help here. They tend to concentrate

on the exposition of biblical books or on the discussion of theological themes. Obviously these are basic concerns, but why is so little
attention paid to the proverbial passages in the Bible or to the
lives of some of the ordinary figures who feature in it? Doctrinal
topics or broader social and political questions, perfectly valid in
themselves, tend to squeeze out more everyday concerns in study
groups. Even work-based Bible studies and study groups rarely
address the specific questions, dilemmas, pressures, and aspirations that arise in the employment situation. In fact, the concentration upon pure Bible study in some of these groups is often an
escape from grappling with the real issues of life.

7. Only occasionally do professional theologians address routine
activities.
I have already identified some of the theological movements which
prepare the ground for (or contain some overlap with) a theology
of everyday life. One way of gauging the general level or professional theological interest in this area is to examine the kind of
papers offered at the main conferences attended by academic theologians. The annual meeting of the Society for Biblical Literature
and American Academy of Religion—with up to 5,000 people attending—provides a good opportunity to sample the level of interest. Over four days of meetings several hundred papers are offered
in a variety of settings.

A sounding I took almost ten years ago turned up less than a
dozen dealing with a subject even remotely connected with the
everyday concerns of ordinary people. Unable, by reason of distance, to attend the conference for a number of years, I did not
take a second sounding until a year or two ago. This was more
heartening. There was a growth in the number of papers that bore
some relation to the everyday affairs. Some of the ethics and
practical theology contributions moved more in this direction.
There was a new section devoted to business ethics. Even so, the
overall character of the conference remained highly technical and
abstruse in character.

While I have no difficultly with scholars working on highly technical or even abstruse subjects, there was an imbalance here
which seemed out of all proportion. Of course, some professional
theologians do write books or articles on down-to-earth matters
for Christians. Some of these writings are also addressed to a

general audience. Topics treated in this way include spirituality, personal relationships, the rites of passage, current moral and social problems. But few academic theologians address the daily struggles, tensions, and situations that the majority of us, and even the majority of them, face. In their writings, says Helmut Thielicke:

> We find men living on esoteric problems which crop up in the theologians' conversations among themselves . . . or they get mired down in methodological considerations and disappear in the smoke of hermeneutics.[10]

The appearance of that last word, hermeneutics — the science or art of interpretation — in a book by one of the best theological communicators this century, is enough to make most people run for cover.

The average Christian — and even the professional theologian — looking for help in an area of practical concern, is more likely to find it in books by non-scholarly authors. A number of these books have good things to say. In some of them there is more contemporary and theological awareness than in the work of many formally trained theologians. Unfortunately, however, a large proportion of non-scholarly Christian books are superficial and misleading. Their grasp of concrete issues is insufficiently informed and their proposals for dealing with them too simplistic. I am not necessarily blaming them for this, for they too are victims of the gap between professional theology and the average Christian that I am discussing. However, it is certainly the shelves containing these books that attract potential buyers rather than the ones filled with contemporary theology titles.

8. When addressed, everyday issues tend to be approached too theoretically.
When I asked a friend of mine, who is a great reader, some time ago why he read so few books by professional theologians, he said: "Because almost none of that kind I have read have the sense of reality I find in books by many of the non-Christian authors that I buy." While his statement may be too extreme, it is not very wide of the mark. Many other Christians feel the same way.

As an inveterate reader myself, I used to find that the appearance of a new theological book by a celebrated writer held a great attraction. I would get hold of such a book as soon as I could and read it at the earliest opportunity. Often I would get through the book in a day or over a weekend, eager to find out whatever insights the author might have. Nowadays some of the magic has gone, partly because I choose to learn more from life at firsthand in a more holistic way than vicariously through another's writings, but partly because I have become increasingly disappointed with the books written by professional theologians, even about more practical concerns.

The trouble with the writings of so many academic theologians, even on matters of common concern, is that they are generally too abstract. They do not get close enough to the ordinary routines of life to see them as they really are. Or, if they do get relatively close, they provide a "still-life" portrait rather than a dynamic analysis. I can think of two reasons for this: sometimes they lack firsthand experience of the issue and are unable to speak about it in concrete terms; sometimes they do not have a sufficient knowledge of the social sciences or contemporary literature to supply a fully rounded description of it. The separation of many theologians from vital involvement in a congregation and the isolation of so much theology from other academic disciplines is part of the problem. But that is not all. We should remember, however, that in many respects academic theology is no worse off than what takes place in most other fields of knowledge.

So I do not want to lay all the blame on professional theologians or on theological institutions. And there are some real exceptions to what I am saying. But from the viewpoint of the average Christian, there is a real lack of integration here. Many professional theologians look at the scene through long-range telescopes, observing some of the same everyday phenomena as others but frequently not seeing the whole picture. Moreover, as a consequence of the particular angle from which they are looking, certain objects have become magnified out of proportion and others are blurred. This is why many people find that the writings of such theologians have an unreal atmosphere about them.

Even where formally qualified theologians are not so out of touch with everyday concerns, another difficulty rears its head. A theological analysis of an issue may be clear and accurate, but what about the prescription for dealing with it? All too often this is very general. Only rarely will the theologian provide an operational model of what might be done and offer practical recommendations or examples drawn from firsthand experience. We are left up in the air, tantalized by a vision of what is possible, but without the means of realizing it. The difficulty here is that most professional theologians are more engaging in talk than action. They are more inclined to interpret reality in the light of revelation rather than do much to actually change it.

9. Only a minority of Christians read religious books or attend theological courses.

Several years ago I was talking with the manager of a Christian bookstore in a large city. He had just completed a piece of market research. To his surprise he found that even among churchgoers only a small percentage ever bought books from such a store. Many more churchgoers bought or borrowed secular books than ever read religious ones. Despite the increase in people signing on for formal courses in theological instruction, the great majority of churchgoers have no interest in these. Some congregations do have a fair proportion of their members involved in study groups. A number of parachurch organizations have also developed their own training programs. In these groups and programs more informal theological learning does go on, but most Christians never take part in such activities. Even those with tertiary qualifications rarely see the need for study, despite their willingness to attend seminars, workshops, and conferences in their own professional field.

In his excellent book *The Function of Theology*, Martin Thornton has something to say about this problem:

It might be suggested that theology is the necessary theory behind religious practice, that it is the mainspring and directive behind practical Christian living. I believe that is, ultimately, the correct answer, but two overwhelming objections to it cannot be evaded. The first is that it does not appear to be so: were this the true answer, then why does not the modern interest in theology in all levels of society manifest itself more obviously? The second objection is that if theology is the necessary theory behind Christian practice, then those most nearly concerned with its nurture and propagation do not appear to think so: ministers of religion form a very small proportion of the theology-reading public.[11]

Most churchgoers regard any kind of theological instruction, formal or informal, as relevant only to a few. It is all right for someone who is training for the ministry or who likes that sort of thing, but they do not feel it has much to offer them. If we look at those people who do read Christian literature or attend theological institutions, we find that they do so mostly for other reasons than developing a Christian understanding of all the routines of life. These people fall into two groups. The first take up theology because they want to understand more about the Bible, doctrine, and church history. This is a worthy aim. The difficulty is that few books and courses of this kind speak the language or address the interests of ordinary Christians. The second group want to develop a Christian perspective on their discipline, occupation, or some special area of concern. Few books and courses emanating from theological institutions deal with these in a direct and practical way. This means that even where some Christians engage in reading and studying theology formally, the gap between professional theology and everyday life remains much as it was.

10. Most churchgoers reject the idea of a gap between their beliefs and their ways of life.
Some time ago I had the opportunity to visit a number of cities for a project enabling them to develop a realistic Christian perspective upon government administration. I did this with a politician from my home city who had been involved in a working group addressing this issue. There was reasonable interest in the topic in most places we visited. But we were not prepared for the reception we received.

Nowhere were we able to assume the premise from which our working group had begun, which was that Christians should make a serious effort to integrate their faith with their work. In each place we visited a number of people took issue with this. They agreed that faith had something to do with their attitude and relationships at work, but not with the actual work itself or the institution in which the work was performed. At points they became quite hostile to any questioning of their position. Only a few people in each place affirmed the link between faith and work that we were advocating. The majority remained fairly quiet, unsure how to respond. Consequently we had to revise our approach to these meetings and begin with fundamentals.

Now if you ask a representative sample of Christians whether faith and life ought to be in harmony, they will answer a resounding "yes." The rub comes when you put the question in a specific way, in relation to a particular aspect of work or area of responsibility. For example, if you are a homemaker and I ask you whether your religious convictions should influence the way you bring up your family and relate to your neighbors, you will probably nod your head in agreement.

But then if I ask you whether those convictions have as clear and direct an influence on the kind of house you have, area you live in, and the means of commuting you use, you will probably pause to think. Unfortunately, we are unaware how much our decisions in these areas are molded by broader social attitudes and have little distinctively Christian about them. Sometimes we are affected by the attitudes and values of our society in these matters as much as people in a totalitarian society are by their country's propaganda machine.

As the Christian educator Douglas Wingeier says:

It is too easy to lay all the blame for our ineptness in doing theology at the door of others. To be sure, the pluralism and individualism of our culture are bewildering, and the attitudes of dependency and dualism cultivated by the church are seductive. But in the final analysis, it is we who either resist or submit to those tendencies. . . . We sense that to try to relate our faith to our daily life would require real effort and courage. We would have to take time to pray, reflect on our experience, and become more familiar with the Bible and Christian beliefs. And we would need to make our through-the-week behavior more consistent with our Sunday affirmations. There could be some risk in this. So, for good reasons, we allow the weeks and years to go by, with the gap between our beliefs and our everyday experience remaining, or growing wider.[12]

We have to recognize this problem and confront it head on. Too much talk about Christian education and a theology of the people assumes that the majority of Christians are simply waiting for the right kinds of books and courses to come along for them to become enthusiastic readers and willing participants in courses that are offered. It would be nice if this were so. But it is just not the case. A minority will respond in that fashion. A number will say that they are interested, but when it comes to the point they will have other things to do. Many will not show much interest at all. Yet some of these are uneasy and can be encouraged to take the matter more seriously. For others, too much is at stake and the only way they will change their mind is by undergoing a radical conversion of their attitudes. But one thing is certain. As Wingeier says, deep down "we know that if we are serious about being full-time Christians, we must make a habit of thinking theologically about our life. If we really want it to make sense again, we must begin doing theology in earnest."[13]

Conclusion

In this chapter I have sought to do two things. First, I have endeavored to show that some Christians are aware of a credibility gap between their beliefs and their everyday lives. Second, I have suggested that professional theology and theological institutions have not done a great deal to overcome this gap. This results in a rather extraordinary situation. The matters which both occupy and preoccupy us the bulk of the time do not receive very much thoughtful Christian consideration. Academic theologians often concern themselves with only a limited range of human experience, leaving much largely unattended. Ordinary Christians often fear the cost involved in integrating their beliefs with their everyday lives.[14]

This is not a happy situation. It leaves too many Christians as divided persons and too much of life out in the cold. It is time we broke out of this captivity and did justice to both belief and everyday life, and linked up these two aspects that God always intended should remain together. It is time to begin *redeeming the routines.*

In the following chapter we shall identify the chief routines we engage in throughout the day or week, as well as the main pressures and features of contemporary life that regularly claim our attention. Our task will be envisioning how these elements can be redeemed in service to Christ.

Questions for Reflection:

1. How do you apply your beliefs to your work? What are two specific changes you think you should make?
2. What should our attitude to leisure be? Draw on your own experience and the information on pages 52 to 54.
3. How can we put the kingdom of God first in our lives when our routine activities place such demands on us?
4. What are examples from your experience of the acquisition impulse, the subtle forms of worldliness, and gray rather than black-and-white moral situations? How can they be dealt with?
5. Consider what may hold you back from a full commitment to Christian belief and behavior. What are some practical steps that can be taken to deal with this?
6. What are some ways we can discuss together everyday matters in church? Are there "non-religious" activities we can do together?
7. Pages 64 to 66 show that there is often a gap between belief and our way of life. What do you think can be done to integrate the two?

THREE
The Texture of Daily Life

Routine aspects of life we need to redeem are of varying kinds. Some arise because of pressures placed upon us by our society; others stem from regular activities in which we are involved. Quite specific questions are raised in the areas of work and leisure, and the central features of modern life bring other issues to the fore. While what follows is fairly detailed, it is not intended to be exhaustive. I am aware that other matters could have been included.

I would like to stress that the following suggestions are not offered apart from careful thought. They distill a considerable amount of personal and family reflection on our own everyday activities. They have been shaped by many hours of conversation with a wide range of people willing to talk about their concerns. They are influenced by experiences people have shared in home churches to which we have belonged. Here and there I have also come across books touching on the subject.

In drawing together the threads from these different encounters, I do not wish to impose upon others my conclusions concerning the issues to which a theology of everyday life should address itself: I am setting out the issues which I see as important. What follows is more of a personal agenda than a prescriptive list. Others' agendas may differ from mine, though I would be surprised if they did not contain many of the same elements. Certainly the actual work of developing a Christian perspective on any one of these issues, or any others that might be framed, can only begin with individuals' declarations of their own concerns.

Some General Social Pressures

Before I discuss a number of crucial social pressures, I suggest that you pause at this point and give some thought to these yourself. What are the major external pressures that surround and affect you? It may take you a little while to do this so do not hurry it. If you are tempted to bypass what I am suggesting here or hurry the process, you might ask yourself why you are inclined to do this.

All societies place pressures upon their members. These pressures are felt by some people more than others but no one entirely escapes their influence: they are too integral a part of life. I believe that the major pressures upon people in our own society are not peculiar to it: we share them, more or less, with all advanced industrial societies. The following are some of the main pressures we experience:

1. Busyness
It is not only the business of life that requires attention but the busyness that so often accompanies it. In this respect a new poverty has emerged in societies like our own over the last two centuries. It is primarily a poverty of the affluent rather than the poor and a hidden poverty rather than one that is immediately recognizable. While a few groups have suffered as a result of this poverty before, it has never occurred on a mass scale as is happening now. We may not be poor economically as the majority of people are in the Two-thirds World, but we are poor in terms of time, whereas they tend to have an abundance of it. What we have gained in terms of material things, we have lost in terms of disposable time. This is especially true of those of us who are middle-class, college-educated, and in professional occupations. Yet it is also true of many migrant or working-class people on low incomes, single-parent families with slender support networks, self-employed people, and working wives who have to fit into others' schedules and patterns. And, because of church and other commitments, Christians are often worse off than others.

The fact of the matter is this: our days are overloaded with too many things to do and never enough time to do them all in. We are whisked along through a kaleidoscope of situations, appointments, activities, and responsibilities for most of our waking hours. However much we try to get ahead, we never seem to catch up. The watch and the pocket planner regulate our time and help us ration it out. We are enslaved to them and feel lost without them. Yet where does all this haste and regulation get us? Our bodies cannot take the pace and malfunction more often. Our nerves are stretched to breaking point and we suffer chronic fatigue. We have little time for family, friends and neighbors. Life ends early for many — through heart attacks and premature death after retirement. Despite sermons on the need to "redeem the time" and our attendance at "time-management" seminars, most of us lack a genuine Christian perspective on our attitude toward and use of time.[1]

2. Mobility

Every year about one in five North Americans have a change of address. A significant percentage of people rarely stay more than two or three years in any one place. Those who are unemployed find it difficult to get permanent work. Those who live on low incomes are not only unable to afford a home, but have to shift regularly from apartment to apartment according to the whims of landlords and rental rates. Even those who have well-paid jobs — indeed, some of those who have top-ranking positions — are involved in a kind of continual migration: within the country, not to it from the outside. Many of us are in danger of becoming nomads, modern gypsies, who never put down firm roots in one place. Such people spend much of their time settling in or preparing to move. Even those who stay five or six years in one place hold back from getting too involved in their community, for they know that one day they will be on the move again. Where Christians are concerned, this is often the case with respect to the church.

Older societies which were too static had their own problems. Mobility brings certain advantages, but too much movement creates other problems and we are now beginning to feel their weight. It breaks up relationships and puts greater pressure upon nuclear family units, pressure under which they frequently crack. It severs people from a sense of place so that they lose touch with their roots and lose sight of the importance of their environment. It cuts them off from certain traditions that would help them negotiate their way more discerningly through life. It curtails their willingness to commit themselves—to other people, to a neighborhood, to institutions—for it is too costly to take that step and then have to withdraw. Apart from occasional challenges to Christians to be ready to launch out into the unknown for God, we lack any substantial Christian appraisal of mobility.[2]

3. Debt

It may sound strange to talk about the pressure of debt when we live in one of the most affluent countries in the world, especially when we have fewer very rich or very poor people here than in most comparable countries. But we are becoming aware of the increasing national debt the United States is accruing and the number of families below the poverty line is also climbing steadily. Such families frequently go into debt because it is the only way they can afford the basic necessities of shelter, food, and clothing. Or, at the very least, they find themselves indebted to various charitable organizations and welfare agencies without whom they could not survive. However, just because many people earn a reasonable amount of money does not mean they are free from debt. On all sides today we are tempted to spend more than we earn. Anyone who has worked in a bank knows how large a proportion of people with very high incomes live from one pay check to the next. Others live off their credit cards and frequently incur such debt that they can do nothing more than meet their "miminum monthly payment" and thus are caught up in a cycle of never paying off their purchases in the required time. Many tie up part of their income in advance through buying items that they cannot afford now and paying for them by installments. In particular, the high cost of housing means that most people are in debt to banks and mortgage or finance companies for up to half their lives. The burden this lays upon young people is quite criminal. Few of us realize how much and for how long enslaved we are in this area.

This situation is unfortunate: first, because we do not examine ourselves more to see how much our own greed produces this situation; second, because we put up with social conditions which automatically sentence people to permanent debt who simply want a home to live in; and third, because some people are ashamed to admit how deeply they are involved in debt and therefore do not call for help when they need it. Owning up to their situation would result in too severe a loss of face.

Debt is also unfortunate because it limits people's options, restricting their freedom to do what God wants until they have paid off their mortgage. Their ability to give to others is likewise circumscribed. Debt is one of the main factors making for tension in the family and for breaking up marriages. Arguments between couples frequently arise over money, or the lack of it. Notions of "thrift" and "saving" were part and parcel of the older middle-class Christian tradition, but this is less so today. Warnings against materialism or against the love of money, and encouragements to give generously, still abound in pulpits. But these in themselves do not amount to an adequate Christian approach to money.

4. Other General Social Pressures in Brief
There are other pressures besides the three already mentioned. Some of these are:
- *Conformity*

During the last century that perceptive critic of emerging forms of democracy, Alexis de Toqueville, issued a warning. He foresaw that democracy's rejection of the tyranny of the one or few could still leave it vulnerable to the tyranny of the many. The preferences and patterns of the majority might increasingly squeeze out minority viewpoints. The role of public opinion polls in marketing and politics and the dominance of the mass media, relying as it does so heavily on advertising, are of concern here. Although in some respects we are now beneficiaries of greater pluralism, there are sufficient signs of tendencies to the contrary to trouble us.
- *Security*

The same writer also argued that, when it came to a crisis or a serious choice, people in the newly emerging democracies would be tempted to place security above freedom. Today, for all our talk of personal independence and regard for civil liberties, we see this happening on an increasing scale. The insurance and banking industries feed on our desire for security, make ever more extravagant claims about their capacity to take care of our future, and advertise their wares in language as religious as any preacher. In an endangered economy we are also watching the way in which those who have are searching for greater guarantees of security for themselves, even if this means providing less justice for those who have not.

● *Regulation*

We are also observing a growing professionalizing and bureaucratizing of life. Aspects of life previously looked after by individuals, families, or voluntary associations have become the preserve of trained specialists. This has not always been to the advantage of the average person. Areas of life generally ignored by governments have also become subject to more administrative regulation. Again, this has not always been beneficial to the wider public. As a consequence, we are in danger of losing the capacity to take responsibility for and manage many of our own affairs.

The pressures I have mentioned are sufficient to indicate some of the forces which shape us and our society. They also shape our churches and Christian organizations far more than we realize. Just think how busy many churches are, how mobile are their members, and how much they are in debt for buildings they have erected. Unless a theology of everyday life comes to terms with pressures like these, it will only scratch the surface of our lives. Our chief need in the face of such pressures is to begin asking questions about them. Often these pressures go unrecognized, or where they do gain recognition are accepted fatalistically. We need to challenge features of our society which so many people take for granted or regard as inevitable. In this area, asking the hard questions, the questions which very few other people are asking, is the beginning of wisdom.

Regular Aspects of Life

Much of life is relatively predictable. Each day presents us with a round of situations to negotiate and most of the time we do this as a matter of course. If we do not spend as much time worrying about these as we do about the pressures we are under, that does not mean they are unimportant. Now and again these matters themselves become problematic. But their significance for us does not rest on this happening. They are significant simply because they are there, an integral part of our lives.

What are some of these regular situations? How fundamental a part do they play in our lives? Do we reflect on them Christianly? Is there a distinctive Christian perspective upon them? Or, if our intentions, motives, and goals are right, will they simply fall into place? Before you read what I have to say, take a sheet of paper and write down the fairly regular or routine activities you engage in on a typical weekday and on a Saturday. Go into detail about this: give thought to what you do every quarter hour of the day and evening. This is what people do who are asked to fill out a time budget survey so that they can know more about where our time goes. Once you have done this, see if you can group your findings under a few general headings that define the broader activities we all take part in.

Now let me list, not in any order of importance, a few of the most common activities we engage in during the course of a day.

1. Commuting

Most of us spend a reasonable amount of time commuting to and from work. By "work" I mean not only the activity of those workers who have to travel to and from their jobs, but those going to school or shopping. It is not generally realized that much of the time gained from shorter working hours or laborsaving devices over the last fifty years has been lost through increased time spent in traveling as cities and suburbs have expanded. Now that a greater percentage of women are in the work force, and those women or men who remain home travel further to shop, more people are traveling more of the time than ever before.

Although we rarely think about it, commuting raises a number of important questions. Is it more important to live closer to work, stores, and schools in less advantageous surroundings so that the family has more opportunity to be together or is quality of place more important? How much energy do people have especially at the start and end of the day, or how much does their mode of transport allow them, to put commuting time to any profitable use? Where it can be used in this way should it be primarily for socializing, catching up with the news, doing additional work, or given over to reading, reflecting, and praying? What can we do about the fact that many of those who can least afford to commute long distances are the ones who often have to do so to find work?

Few people have given much thought to the effect of different kinds of transportation on our society as a whole.[3] The advantages of the car are well known and I do not need to labor them here. Nor would I want what follows to be interpreted as a plea for doing away with it. But it is society's adoption of the car that has been the main contributor to the deterioration of mass public transportation over the last fifty years. Do we not have a responsibility here to older, younger, poorer, and disabled people who rely on public transportation? While a car may be necessary for some people most of the time and for all of us some of the time, should you limit the number of cars your household runs and have a practical commitment to carpooling? Do you really need a car at all, or can you make do with part-ownership of a car with other members of your family or church?

Since the automobile is one of the main causes of accidents and deaths in our advanced Western society—with figures now climbing toward 50,000 deaths and 500,000 injuries in the United States annually—how do we fulfill our responsibility to minimize this carnage? Given that the car is the chief contributor to pollution of the atmosphere, what practical steps can we take to combat this? How effectively do Christians resist the wide scale idolatry of the car in our society or allow worldly values in this area to mold them into its own image? How justified is it to go into debt to purchase a car and would the money spent on the car—around one quarter of the average person's income—be better employed in other ways? What effect would a drop in the purchase of cars have upon employment in the automobile industry and how far should this influence our decisions in this area?

2. Shopping

If we are to go by the amount of money spent upon advertising, then shopping is perhaps the central activity around which our society revolves. The amount of effort we put into thinking about what to buy is one indicator of this. Shopping is one of our main topics of conversation. Families spend more time on shopping trips than on enjoyment of nature or going to church. By their own admission, newspapers, radio, and television primarily exist to advertise goods and services rather than provide news, entertainment, and education. Around 75 percent of newspaper space is given over to advertisements, while commercial radio and television programming is a battle to gain advertisers rather than viewers.

The size and character of the buildings now being constructed for shopping is another sign of its importance. Shopping malls are the new cathedrals of the suburbs, increasingly dominating the geography, roadways, socializing, and politics of local communities.

Economic considerations dominate these complexes, and big companies control much of what goes on inside them. Yet to some extent such malls do provide space for people to gather and for communal activities to take place, just as the media do give us some access to news and information and provide a certain degree of enjoyable entertainment. Buying and selling are also valid activities in themselves and have helped improve not just the quantity but also the quality of life in certain respects.

From one angle, shopping has been accorded substantial Christian attention. For more than a decade, advocates of a simpler lifestyle have challenged people to question their consumer-orientated outlook.[4] Adopting a lower standard of living, they have argued, would help overcome the gap between the poor and the wealthy both within and between countries. It would also result in a better quality of life for those who took this step. But the principle of "enough is enough" has only gone skin-deep into Christian consciousness and the "simple lifestyle" analysis does not penetrate sufficiently deeply into the manipulative character, addictive nature, and quasi-religious appeal of shopping in our society.

People in marketing and advertising work hard to break down our resistance to the lure of shopping. The architecture, layout, color scheme, and atmosphere of shopping malls are all carefully calculated to entice us to spend. They are also designed to take us out of ourselves, transcend our routine lives, and give us a sort of religious experience. (In recognition of the role of shopping in our culture, one innovative congregation — Leith Anderson's Wooddale Church — recently held a Sunday worship service at the newly opened Mall of America in Bloomington, Minnesota, site of the largest mall in the United States, in an attempt to contextualize the Gospel.[5]) Through the clothes they buy people are sometimes searching for their own identity or trying to create one they do not have. The quest for bargains and discounts partly arises from a desire to receive something gratuitously, as a matter of "grace" so to speak. The big purchases people make often stem from the unconscious longing for a "peak experience" that will bring them a sense of well-being.[6] Quite apart from all this, some people — mainly retired, deserted, and disadvantaged people — live under the weekly pressure of not having enough money to buy the things that they need. Further, they are often seduced to buy the wrong things or spend beyond what their income permits.

3. Sleeping

At the beginning of this book I mentioned the importance of developing a theology of sleep. We need to do this partly because so much of our lives are taken up with sleep. But sleep is important in itself. It is not just a withdrawal from activity. Important physical, psychological, and spiritual processes are at work while we are lying in bed. Alongside the physical rest our bodies benefit from in sleep, we all dream much more than we suppose. Unless we did so we would be unable to cope with waking life. Dreams enable us to absorb and come to terms with many of the events we have encountered during the day. Some of these dreams reveal aspects of ourselves which our conscious mind will not admit. God also reveals to us through dreams — or sometimes by means of a vision or voice — things He wishes us to know and to do. The Bible is full of such incidents. So are the lives of people in non-Western societies. It is only those in Western society who discount the importance of these phenomena or who have lost the capacity to interpret them.

Other thoughts are prone to come to our minds before we go to sleep at night or before we get up in the morning. Sometimes in these rare moments of quiet we are put in touch with our deepest longings and receive hints about our basic vocation. Others lie awake planning and plotting to their own advantage, sometimes even masking this with a veneer of spirituality, rather than entrusting themselves in sleep to God. Many people, and you may be one of them, find it difficult to sleep properly today. This may stem from the amount of work you choose to do and the hectic pace at which you live. It may stem from the amount of work you are forced to do and the number of responsibilities you have to carry. Insomnia is now the most widespread disability in Western countries and is seriously affecting people's physical, emotional, mental, and spiritual capacities. We need to identify not only its personal and social causes, as certain writers are already doing, but its spiritual roots as well. The Bible has something to say about this, in passages which are often overlooked or deliberately ignored (e.g., Gen. 41:1-32; Pss. 4:8; 127:1-2; Prov. 6:22; Dan. 6:18).

4. Other Regular Aspects of Daily Life

I have considered only three repetitive aspects of life that require serious Christian consideration. There are many others. Let me briefly mention a number of more specific activities:

- *Eating and drinking*

The nature, enjoyment, and purpose of cooking; the role of meals in family life; the importance of hospitality; the religious dimension of the ordinary meal; the vulgarization of eating and drinking in modern society; the meal as an expression of our concern for, and inclusion of, the lonely and needy; the role of traditional extended family meals, such as birthdays and Christmas; the rejuvenation of wider and narrower family celebrations.

- *Dress*

The problem of fashion—dress as a status symbol in modern society; the problem of mass conformity—and mass non-conformity—in dress; the exploitation of workers in the clothing industry; the significance of homemade as well as shop-bought clothes; the extent to which clothes should be an expression of the individual; the extent to which clothes should be an indicator of public function; the use of clothes for sexual differentiation or titillation; the inordinate amounts of money spent on clothing; the validity or invalidity of regimentation of clothing in some institutions; the need to do away with distinctions of dress in the church.

- *Hospitality*

Importance of people having a space of their own into which they can invite others; the gift of hospitality as one of the manifestations of the Spirit and ways in which it can be developed; the reasons for the contraction of hospitality in our society; the problem of homelessness among the young, refugees, and physically abused; the ministry of hospitality to the lonely, the disadvantaged, and the ostracized; the role of hospitality in evangelism in the early church and today; the home as the basic location for gathering as church; home designing and decoration as a context for people's art; the role of communal living or of including in your home one who has no close family relationships.

- *Hobbies*

The rise of the hobby as a compensation for the monotony of work; the relationship between the hobby and leisure; the mass production of hobbies and the demise of the self-created activity; the hobby as an escape from family and social responsibilities; the hobby as the development of a creative gift and how to stimulate it in those whom society views as failures.

- *Gardening*

The link between God's creation of and care for the world and gardening; gardening as a means of retaining a link with nature in an urban environment; gardening as fulfilling a responsibility to future generations; the temptation to turn gardening into an all-absorbing preoccupation; the garden as a context for parables from God; the possibilities in gardening for sharing with the poor; gardening as a self-help task for the retired and unemployed; the importance of public gardens in an urban or suburban landscape; the implications of the importance of gardens for housing policy and housing developments.

On Work and Leisure

1. Work

Once again I am using the word *work* in a wider sense than is usually understood. Work embraces:

- paid employment,
- housework,
- schoolwork and study,
- voluntary work,

and we need a theology of all these. Here again you might like to think first what you would list here if you were writing this section. Go over in your mind your own work situation, whatever that might be, and try to define the main issues that it raises for you. Some of these might arise out of your own choice or circumstances, others might be forced upon you by those whom you work for, or be felt as outside impositions even by them. When you have done this, see how similar or different your lists are.

It is now clear that the more people spend their time in a certain environment the more they will be shaped by that environment. In our kind of society, the work environment is, for some, the most total and life-encompassing institution, often more so than the family. It is where many find their identity, status, and power. It significantly affects their views and values. The influence of the work environment explains why people who have similar occupations so often think, talk, behave, and even dress alike. Since work is the main reality for many of us, we test much else that we experience by judgments we form through it. As yet, we have scarcely begun to come to terms with the all-pervasive effect that the work environment has on the way most of us look at life and

conduct ourselves. As we have seen, it can even modify or undermine religious beliefs and values.

Here are some of the questions we need to address:

• How can work, wherever it takes place, become a less secu-
larizing experience? What can be done to help Christians compart-
mentalize their lives less between church and work or between
their inner and outer selves at work?

• What should motivate our choice of a particular occupation?
Should it be motivated by a sense of meaningfulness, fulfillment,
service, ministry? How far should we be influenced by education
results, others' pressure, financial reward, or status considerations?

• Where do those who wish to conduct their work in a more
responsible way find the resources and support to do this?

• How possible is it to develop a set of standards for occupations, professions, companies, industries, or departments that will
meet with common consent?

• What should employers and what can employees do about the
unreal pressures and expectations which exist in so much paid
employment?

• How far is excellence and promotion an achievable and desir-
able goal and to what extent are the two compatible?

• What are the limits to our obedience and accountability to our
employers and what are their responsibilities to their employees?

• How do we deal with the problem of abusive and discrimina-
tory language at work, double standards, favoritism, and obstruc-
tionism, or peer pressure to do less work than is appropriate?

• What is the responsibility of Christians who belong to a union
in terms of seeking office in it, responding to calls for passive or
militant action, and making their opinions felt when unions appear
to go too far or not far enough?

• What responsibility do Christian employers and employees
have to discover creative, perhaps even unpopular, ways of gener-
ating new jobs and alleviating the unemployment problem?

• How can we encourage people to see their work in the context of God's providential ordering of life in the world and discover
the implications of this for organizations, household, and
individuals?

• Are the churches themselves at the forefront of pioneering
new approaches to work that will lead people into new patterns

and types of worthwhile activity, even if these are voluntary in nature and outside the structures of paid employment?

• How can we give people a sense of the value of their work irrespective of the amount they are paid for it?

• Can housework be integrated into a genuinely Christian vision of life that does not idolize or belittle it, entertain myths about technology's time-saving contribution, or restrict it to the woman's sphere.

• How harmful or beneficial is it, by means of the emphasis upon homework, to inculcate into children the idea of bringing work home at the end of the day?[7]

Once again I am not trying to be exhaustive. There are other questions that could be asked about the size of many work environments, such as bureaucracies. How much power should be given to those bureaucracies, such as multinational corporations, which are based abroad or to associations of people involved in work, such as trade unions? From your own experience of work I am sure that you could add other questions to this list.

Happily, some of these issues are now being addressed by Christian thinkers and writers, as well as by small groups of Christians in their workplaces. This is beginning to provide a broader definition of what we should regard as work and a clearer understanding of how we should view and do our work.[8] We are also beginning to see a more concerted effort to analyze and combat a related problem, large scale unemployment. In some measure this is now here to stay and there is no simple solution to it. It will be a fact of life well into the future and we have to prepare ourselves and our children for it, as well as find ways of minimizing it where we can. There is a need for experiment in this area, as well as reflection if we are to make any substantial inroads into the problem.

2. Leisure

Following is a list of some high priority leisure pursuits: walking, rock climbing, hiking, board games, team sports, swimming, boating, picnicking, camping, travel, and tourism. For only one of these do I know of a carefully and joyously developed theological appraisal.[9]

For most people leisure is a central part of their lives. This is still true, even if working hours have tended to increase in recent years. African-Americans and Hispanic-Americans maintain it as a priority. A large proportion of West Coast Canadians and Americans likewise prefer increased leisure time to higher income. While in parts of North America many people live in order to work, many others work in order to live. For some years now, forecasters have predicted the arrival of the "leisure society." Urban planners and companies have conducted many surveys to find out what we might want to do with the extra time at our disposal. We can also take courses to prepare us to use our leisure constructively. For some time state governments have been hiring directors of sports and recreation to develop these more fully. Local governments increasingly seek to provide for the leisure needs of the young people in their district.

Yet most people have less leisure than they are told to imagine. The rhythms of work carry over into their leisure time so that they cannot really enjoy it as they would like. I have also noted that economic circumstances or social disadvantages sometimes prevent people from experiencing the leisure they need. There is an ongoing tendency to turn leisure activities into things at which people work hard or through which they feel pressured. We have also watched the growth of giant leisure industries to cater to our wants in this area. Leisure has become a multibillion dollar industry which carefully manipulates the way in which we spend our free time. There are many issues that require attention here. I invite you to enumerate those which occur to you.

Beyond the issues I have already raised in connection with sports and recreation, I list the following:

• From a Christian point of view, do we work primarily to have leisure or have leisure primarily to refresh ourselves for work?

• What is leisure anyway, and how far does it overlap with or differ from what we describe as "free time"?

• How much real "rest" do people get during their time off from work?

• Is "play" equivalent to "sports" and, if not, what kind of balance should be struck between the two?

• Have many sporting activities become more competitive and how much is this a good thing?

• How much should we encourage children to engage in non-competitive games as opposed to competitive sports?

• How self-initiating or technologically dependent, and how

spontaneous or programmed, should leisure activities be?

• What balance should be struck between appreciating the creation around us and developing the creative gifts we have been given?

• Do weekend church activities help or hinder the "rest" the Bible encourages us to enjoy?

• Where do meditation and contemplation fit in to time spent in leisure?

• How much should leisure be a corporate and not merely individual or family affair? How much should church members play together?

• How can the Sabbath principle or inner rest which God enjoys be more fully experienced by and made available to Christians?

These are by no means the only questions that need to be pursued. For example, how much should governments be permitted to spend on producing elite athletes rather than making provisions for all people to engage in some sport? How can pressure be brought to bear so that control of the media is decentralized and greater access given to a range of community and other groups? Other issues include the way in which vacations can be most fruitfully taken and the role of the sabbatical year or extended leave of absence in discovering where one is heading in life. There is also the major question of retirement in a society in which people are increasingly living longer. This is a vast area in itself and one that needs more and more of our attention. The provision of church homes and services for the aged is a real contribution here. But it is only the outer edge of a large tract of unexplored territory.[10]

Central Features of Modern Life

I would now like to discuss several important aspects of modern life which we do well to understand and confront. Since these are more diffuse in character than the matters I have mentioned to this point, it would be more difficult to ask you to test your own perceptions against mine. Again I will only refer to a number of areas and briefly indicate why I think each is important.

1. Popular attitudes and values
We have many statistical studies of the attitudes and values of

ordinary North Americans. These are helpful to a point, but they do not go very deep. Only in-depth interviews begin to reveal the full character of people's outlooks, the actual strength of their convictions; and the complex, paradoxical, and even contradictory nature of many of their views. Public opinion polls, census figures, studies, and values surveys can only take us so far. They give us a surface reading of what we as a people are thinking, choosing, and doing. But we need more than this. There are quite simple yet profound questions we can all ask. What are the things that make the average person in our society:

- laugh and cry?
- hope and despair?
- believe and doubt?
- share and withdraw?
- love and hate?
- trust and fear?

The only place to begin here is with ourselves and with those closest to us. I know of no better way to begin to know ourselves and others more closely, and we will find out things by this means that no survey or commentator can discover.[11]

Even when we have a fuller picture of what is going on inside the minds, hearts, and imaginations of ordinary North Americans, the hardest work is still to be done. We need to know how to bring the light of the Gospel to bear upon their:

- images of reality,
- the motives they live by,
- the values they live by,
- the beliefs they entertain,
- the goals they have.

These are difficult questions to answer. While some attention has been given to these cross-cultural values and practices, we still know too little.[12] And such interpretations tend to be either too individual or purely sociological in character. In both areas we have taken only a few steps down what is a rather long road.

2. Communicating and relating

Communication takes place in a number of different ways in our society. Apart from the not unimportant nonverbal forms of communication, there is:

- conversation,

- discussion,
- instruction,
- letter writing,
- telephoning,
- reading,
- mass media.

With the exception of the third and the last, we do not have any developed Christian understanding of these.

Relating and communicating also go on in different contexts, defined by the places or spaces we inhabit. These also require consideration, especially settings in which genuine relationships are forged and real communication goes on. I am thinking here of:

- the house or apartment,
- the street or neighborhood,
- the mall or restaurant,
- the workplace or club,
- the park or center,
- the campsite or vacation site,

as well as more intermittent meetings, such as while traveling.

There are a number of issues connected with communication that we need to address. Given the prevalence of superficial media presentations and unexamined peer group opinions, how far are we succumbing to propaganda and prejudices rather than forming properly thought-out views? What about the fact that less powerful groups in society — ethnic groups, native peoples, the aged — do not get as much representation as others? How high on our agenda, even in Christian families and churches, is the creation of space for informed and critical conversation on matters of importance? How much time or energy do we have at the end of a day or over a weekend to read the material that would help us form sound judgments about a whole range of matters? These are only some of the questions we should be asking and answering. For we are in real danger in our universally educated society of producing people who are uninformed about many of the major issues that affect our lives.

As we are all aware, relationships are under stress in our society. Marriages are breaking up at an ever increasing rate, parents and children are seeing less and less of one another as each group pursues its own self-fulfillment, individuals in peer groups are becoming more narcissistic, and friends find it hard to clear time to enjoy each other's company in regular and leisurely ways. Symptoms of this deterioration are not difficult to identify. One example is the decline in letter writing, especially of long, reflective letters to people at a great distance, something which long distance telephone calls can only partly replace.

There has also been a demise in extended day-, weekend- or vacation-long visits between friends. In fact we need to revivify the whole notion of friendship for it is in serious danger of becoming superficial. The problem of lack of communication within marriage or among families is happily better served from a Christian point of view, though even much of what is said fails to come to grips with the realities of married life and with the effects of changes in working, social, and urban patterns upon couples and children today.

3. Social Rituals and Activities

There are a number of rituals in our society about which there has been very little Christian reflection. Think, for example, of the following:
  • *Enforced Waiting*
One of the ironies of our society, which is obsessed with speed, is the amount of time we spend waiting, queuing, or sitting in traffic jams. Waiting is one of our least acknowledged rituals. If we do spend up to 5 percent of our lives waiting for one reason or another, surely we ought to have some understanding of why this happens, what we can do about it, and how or whether we should spend the time more fruitfully.
  • *Family Events*
We still tend to celebrate family events such as birthdays, engagements, and anniversaries in conventional ways without giving much thought to how they could be enhanced Christianly. Other events such as the birth of children, obtaining a job, moving to another city, the purchase of a house, coming-of-age, and retirement are rarely celebrated in a way that does them justice from a Christian point of view.
  • *Popular Rites*
Weekly rituals, like an evening shopping trip or weekend outing to the mall, are often a family affair. What is or is not going on when this is taking place and how much does it enhance our lives or replace more significant family rituals? Eating out is another well-

known ritual, replacing home-based hospitality as a way of entertaining others. There are also those culturally legitimate opportunities for gambling—connected with betting, casinos, and lotteries—that so attract sections of the population. Do we know why these are so popular and how much they symbolize the main forces and preoccupations in our society? Do we know what will most attract others to put their risk-taking instincts to more constructive use?

• *Club Membership*

Social clubs are very popular in modern society. They range from large clubs centered on sports, nationality, or military veterans to the small associations based on some hobby or interest. Yet clubs also existed in large numbers in the first century. The early Christians had come to terms with them, as passages in the New Testament bear witness. How do we understand, evaluate, and respond to the phenomenon of the club? In what ways do clubs make a social contribution or harmfully influence their members? What possibilities do they offer for communicating the Gospel or gathering as church? We might also consider how far congregations have themselves become simply religious clubs.

• *Civic Celebrations*

Apart from church services associated with particular ceremonies, and occasional participation by Christians in city festivals, how much have we thought about involving ourselves in such happenings? We are part of a larger community and from time to time should celebrate what we have in common. Should we perhaps seek ways of enhancing civic occasions? So many of them turn most people into spectators and we could help make them more participatory. How can we as congregations celebrate and—in view of our treatment of Native Americans—lament the founding of our nation? We have hardly any traditions to follow here.

4. Secular Idols and Religions

In the West we have a particular fascination with objects. In fact, we tend to value things more than people. Some of the objects are central to the operation of our society and therefore become symbols of what we most highly prize. These objects receive an enormous amount of attention. They are the locus of a whole range of expectations. Yet they are also a source of frustration and have many disruptive and harmful effects. In other words they have all the characteristics of *idols*. If the following items were not so difficult to avoid noting as you read this, I would suggest that you make your own list and compare it with mine. I doubt whether there would be many differences. These are the ones that came to my mind, most of them fairly readily:

- the watch,
- the daily planner,
- the credit card,
- the telephone,
- the computer,
- the television/VCR,
- the car,
- the home.

For all their centrality in modern life, all these but the last have received surprisingly little attention from Christian thinkers. I have written at length about some of these—the watch, daily planner, and telephone—elsewhere.[13] I have also said something about others—the credit card and car—earlier in this book. The television set and the computer have received, or are beginning to receive, thoughtful Christian attention.[14] While I have mentioned the home briefly already, in connection with debt, I would like to add a little here.

The home occupies a special place in our lives. It is part of the North American dream. But many people can no longer afford a home and even rented accommodations are becoming less available or less permanent. Others are being turned out of their homes and have nowhere to live. We are seduced into thinking that a satisfying life is impossible unless we own a home that accords with the latest expectations and sacrifice more of our money, time, and energy to it than we give to other people or needs. We turn it into a monastic retreat from the world rather than a creative bridgehead into it. We think individualistically about it and do not consider ways in which we can cooperate in designing, financing, building, and living in homes that have a more modest and more communal character. Our decisions in this area often result in unnecessary delay in having children, unfortunate clustering in more advantaged parts of our cities, and increasing already congested traffic patterns.

In varying degrees, all the objects I have mentioned, allowing for the many benefits they have bestowed upon us, threaten to shape us more than we control them. They are significant pointers to the main substitute religions. Although these substitute religions are fairly well known, too often we merely denounce them, failing to see that we are often caught up in them ourselves. These religions are:

- material possessions,
- guaranteed security,
- the family,
- educational achievement,
- work and sports,
- fitness and health,
- self and sexual fulfillment.

The extent to which Christians are vulnerable to these substitute religions is a matter for careful reflection. Even though they might attempt to resist crasser pressures to become consumer-oriented, Christians are easily tempted to join the treasure hunt for the best discounts, sales, and clearances and turn these into a central feature of their thinking and conversation. They are in danger of treating the nuclear family as an idol, neglecting the biblical role of the extended natural family or extended Christian family, of the church within the church. Christians are as vulnerable as anyone to loading expectations upon their children about educational advancement through the "best" schools, despite the pressure it brings upon the need for both parents to work and the effect this often has on the quality of family life.

Though Christians may have repudiated any approach to God based on justification by works, they can easily be caught up in an attempt to prove their worth and acceptability to others and themselves, even partially to God, through their work. Keeping healthy and fit is entirely proper, especially in our chair-bound and car-imprisoned society, but there is always a danger of giving more time and attention to this than to our relationships—with God as well as with others. So pervasive is the belief that happiness is one of the goals we should have in life, that it is almost impossible for us to escape altogether the feverish search for self-fulfillment, especially if it is cloaked in the language of charismatic experiences or spiritual exercises. So then, while all these aspects of life are legitimate in themselves, we must exercise care lest they become ends in themselves rather than means, and not necessarily means for all of us, toward other more fundamental ends.

Conclusion

I would like to give the concluding word to Jacques Ellul who, more than anyone writing at present, has made the most trenchant plea for every aspect of our lives to be drawn into a Christian pattern of understanding:

It is evident that the first thing to do is to be faithful to revelation, but this fidelity can only become a reality in daily life through the creation of a new way of life: this is the "missing link." There used to be a style of life peculiar to the Middle Ages. In the sixteenth century there was a style of life carried on by Reformed Church Christians, and it is extremely interesting to note where it differed from the style of life of the Renaissance. There is the bourgeois style of life, which has no spiritual quality at all; there is the Communist style of life; there is no longer a Christian style of life. To speak quite frankly, without beating about the bush, a doctrine only has power (apart from that which God gives it) to the extent to which it creates a style of life, to the extent to which it is adopted, believed and accepted by people who have a style of life which is in harmony with it. . . .

If we consider the life of Christians in our churches, we see certainly that they make good sons, fathers, husbands, employers and workmen. They have many individual virtues but they have no style of life, or rather, they have exactly that which has been imposed upon them by their sociological conditions: that is to say, by their social class, their nation, their environment and so on. It is not their spiritual condition which affects their style of life: it is their political or economic condition, and from this point of view, they are an overwhelming demonstration of the truth, temporary and temporal, of Marxism. Now at the present time, many Christians are fully aware that this is an intolerable situation, and that if it is allowed to go on, it will prepare the way for the total collapse of the churches in the West. The problem of the style of life is absolutely central: for it is at this point that the question of the integration of Christianity into the world, or at least of its creative power, will be most fiercely tested. . . .

The creation of such a style of life is a work which is both collective and individual. It is a fact for each Christian who really tries to express his faith in the concrete forms of his life. It is also the task of Christians as a corporate body, where all these efforts, sometimes differing widely, sometimes even contradictory, are recorded . . . as its name indicates, the whole of life is concerned in this search. It includes the way we think about present political questions, as well as our way of practicing hospitality. It also affects the way we dress and the food we eat (. . . the problems of taste, fashion, cooking, are important if we are to form a style of life . . .) as well as the way in which we manage our financial affairs. It includes being faithful to one's wife as well as being accessible to one's neighbor. It includes the position one ought to take on current social questions, as well as the decisions which relate to the personal employment of our time.

I could multiply these examples, which are mere suggestions, to show that absolutely everything, the smallest details which we regard as indifferent, ought to be questioned, placed in the light of faith, examined from the point of view of the glory of God.[15]

In this chapter I have identified some of the routine situations, pressures, and features of life today that we need to approach with greater understanding. As I have stressed throughout, these are not the only aspects of everyday life that require consideration. In particular I have said little about some of the life stages people pass through—from birth, through marriage to death—and some of the moral dilemmas that people face from time to time—divorce, abortion, homosexuality—many of which are discussed in works of pastoral or applied theology. These areas of concern do form part of the wider Christian consciousness, and in recent times there have been some excellent treatments of them. I have also said little about some of the social issues which are important today—racial discrimination, unemployment, and poverty—and some of the political threats which overhang us—government centralization and nuclear extinction. But that is because these issues are already receiving some attention by Christian thinkers, and much of the time there is less we can do about these directly than many of the matters I have mentioned.

This leads us to the next stage of our investigation. Now that we have some appreciation of the wide range of everyday issues that invite and require our thoughtful Christian attention, how do we go about realistically addressing them? What avenues are open to us and how, given the demands and responsibilities most Christians already experience, can we hope to pursue them in an effective way? These concerns form the substance of the following chapter.

Questions for Reflection:

1. What part do busyness, mobility, and debt play in your life?
2. "We need to challenge features of our society which so many people take for granted or regard as inevitable" (page 76). How can conformity, security, and regulation be challenged?
3. Make a list of the routine duties you do each day. Are they all necessary? Are there better ways to organize them? How can you be *redeeming the routines* of everyday life?
4. Look at the questions on commuting on pages 77 to 78. If you are a commuter, what changes would you like to make?
5. The author refers to "the wide-scale idolatry of the car" (page 78). What is the car's proper and improper role in our lives?
6. Take *one* of the five routine aspects of life mentioned on pages 81 to 82 and list four or five questions that you think are important about it from a Christian viewpoint.
7. "Since work is the main reality for many of us, we test much else that we experience by judgments we form through it" (page 82). Is work your main reality? What affect does it have on the rest of your life?
8. How can our social rituals and activities (pages 89 to 90) be more Christian?
9. How can the home become a substitute religion?
10. "A doctrine only has power . . . to the extent to which it creates a style of life" (page 93). Do you agree? What do you find helpful in the statement on pages 93 to 94 by Jacques Ellul?

FOUR
The Reality Principle

I have identified certain aspects of everyday life that we could attend to more closely. How is it possible for any individual, you might ask, to deal with all these issues? Where do I find the time? What should have priority for me? How do I cope in the meantime with not being able to work through other matters? It will help if you bear two things in mind.

First, we do not have to tackle these issues on our own. In fact, it is impossible for us to do so. Only if we tackle them with others will we find the wisdom and strength to do so. Alone they will prove too much: together they are manageable, not only because we will get further if we work together, but because different ones among us will work at different issues so that each one does not have to grapple with all. To do this, however, we have to overcome that individualism which infects our society. It is because we expect to have to do everything ourselves that we are sometimes overwhelmed by all that there is to do.

Second, we do not have to find answers right away. We tend to want quick answers to our questions, but they are often superficial. It takes time to discern the truth and we should not feel under pressure about this, certainly not from God. He has structured us so that in all aspects of our life—physically, emotionally, intellectually, and spiritually—we take time to reach maturity. So we should take the long-term view and be content with the small but regular progress we are able to make. In any case we will intuitively find answers to some of our questions in the area of everyday life long before we can put these into words. Sometimes our thinking is behind our acting and we know more than we can tell.

But we do need criteria in order to select which issues we should concentrate on. What are these criteria? I think there are two basic ones. First, if as Christians we are seeking to serve our families, friends, fellow Christians, and others, what is most relevant to them? Second, what is most relevant to us, at this moment? These two questions will not only provide us with a starting point, but will provide new issues as we go along.

The next question to be tackled is: Where can we best do this? This opens up a number of related issues. Which contexts for learning are the most suitable? How much or how little structure do we require? To what extent can existing patterns of Christian and theological education provide what is needed? Who will develop new models and what should they look like?

There are also a number of practical issues. Should we take time to reflect on everyday matters while continuing our regular commitments, or should we also take extended time out from these routines so we can give them more concentrated attention? Who can provide us with the basic resources that we need—those with formal theological qualifications or those with practical wisdom in the area under discussion? What group processes are best designed to take us where we wish to go? How much do we require a supportive as well as a thoughtful group to enable us to do this?

These are not the only issues to consider, but they are some of the most important. Unless we take them seriously, existing methods and attitudes will prevail by default. This would be a pity, if only because such methods and attitudes are not adequate to attain their own stated goals. In what follows I shall suggest a variety of ways in which we can develop more appropriate structures and attitudes that are more conducive to developing a Christian approach to everyday life. All of them have been worked out and put into practice. Some have sprung out of my own work and I have seen others at firsthand or been involved in them.

The Value of Churching at Home

Involvement in a house church or basic Christian community— whether within a congregation or not—can make a significant contribution to developing a Christian understanding of everyday life. I have already mentioned that my interest in home churches partly developed out of the search for a form for the church which brought it closer to everyday life. For me there is a direct connection between the two. As we shall see, others have come to the same conclusion through starting from the problems of everyday life and searching for a corporate way of resolving them.

Since the word is used so loosely today, I need to define what I mean when I say *house church*. I have in mind small, informal extended Christian family units which meet for church in a home. Sometimes these are independent of any denomination, sometimes they belong to one. Whatever the case, those who gather in homes for church also gather regularly in a larger meeting, either with a cluster of independent home churches every so often or every week with other members of their congregation.[1] What does involvement in a house church have to do with thinking Christianly about everyday life? And why have I begun with reference to this? The best way to explain this is to draw on the experience of William Diehl who became increasingly aware of the gap between his religious and workaday worlds while he was a senior executive in a major U.S. steel corporation. He also regretted the fact that his church had not helped him to bridge this gap. Toward the end of his book, *Christianity and Real Life*, Diehl describes how he began to find an answer:

> In recent years a form of local grouping has emerged. We call it the "house church" and it is almost universally a lay-initiated phenomenon. . . . The name of our house church is *Focus* . . . it consists of twenty-three adults and twenty children. Six of the families are active members in traditional church parishes representing three denominations. Seven of the families formerly were active in the church, but dropped out due to the failure of their congregations to provide the kind of support they felt was necessary in relating faith to life today. . . . There are two former clergymen in the group, but their role is the same as that of any other member in the group. In areas of biblical knowledge they do have more expertise, but then our scientist members have greater skills in their respective fields also. Those families which are still associated with the institutional church all agree that *Focus*

has provided their lives with a dimension of Christian community which they have been unable to find in their traditional congregations.

The general operational style of *Focus* has changed very little during the past five years. Every other Sunday morning the total community gathers at the faculty house of a local college for breakfast and a worship-study period. Families take turns providing the simple breakfast and leading the morning program. . . . Worship in the Focus community is relevant to the real-life experiences of the group and springs from the innermost thoughts and concerns of all its members. The educational period, which is woven into or follows the worship experience, is also designed by the same parents and children. Generally, a theme has been established by the community to extend over several sessions. For example, over a period of several months we studied various families in the Bible, with each of us selecting a favorite Bible family and presenting a learning session on it. Frequently, the educational periods involve such things as role-playing, small group discussion, skits, and use of visual aids. Efforts are made for the study periods to have an experiential dimension to them. . . .While these learning periods may lack the comprehensive content of institutionally designed curriculum material, they far exceed parish religious education experiences in freshness, excitement, and total involvement of people. . . . I believe the example we set before our children as we struggle to learn about our faith and share it with the rest of the community is a far more enduring type of learning than that which most children get in their parish Sunday schools.

On alternate Sunday evenings, the adult members of *Focus* gather in a home for discussion, study, sharing of life experiences, and providing of mutual support. At times the group may review a religious book or essay. Sometimes there will be a series of evenings devoted to study of topics of current interest. . . . The style of our evenings together is such that the agenda can readily be switched to that which is needed by one of the members. A member of the community is thus free to bring up anything that is happening in his or her life which he or she would like to share with friends. . . . Not only are individuals able to share their concerns with the rest of

the group, they can rely on support from the other members.
... Thus the sharing of family problems, of job concerns, of
town and neighborhood service efforts, or of other personal
experiences provides effective support and love for the individual members unlike anything I have ever experienced in a
traditional congregation.[2]

Diehl concludes by emphasizing that the house church phenomenon is a grass-roots response to the credibility gap between belief
and daily life that many Christians experience. It is a "bottom-up"
rather than "top-down" affair, one discovered and designed for the
most part by ordinary Christians themselves. He points out that it
is also an informal rather than formal approach to the problem,
which allows people's own experiences to dictate the agenda and
for learning to take place through group discussion and study. He
stresses the importance of the "supportive" as well as more specifically "educational" character of the group, for translating faith
into action also requires others' encouragement and prayers. Such
a group also has a unique contribution to make to character formation, which is vital since the mere acquisition of knowledge is not
sufficient of itself to alter behavior patterns. For these and other
reasons, I am convinced that some kind of home church experience is fundamental to developing an integrated Christian approach to life.
    Other study groups or action groups can produce some of the
same benefits, but they are less holistic in their effects and do not
tend to create the same climate of trust and promote the same
level of sharing of day-to-day situations. Where you cannot belong
to a house church, such groups are a partial compensation. Occasionally membership in two groups, one a close support group and
one a practical study group, can provide a measure of the same
experience. Where you wish to belong to a house church but do
not know of one you can join, you might think of starting one,
either in your own congregation or among people who attend different local churches. In itself belonging to a home church is not
enough. As I shall go on to explain, we need to place ourselves in
other learning contexts as well if we wish to bring our faith to bear
upon *redeeming the routines* of life in an effective way. Where it is
possible to do so, however, linking up with a home church is the
best starting point.

One Role Model Is Worth 100 Instructions

We learn the most fundamental things in life by having them modeled to us by significant others. Often we are not aware how much we do learn this way. We are not always conscious how much we are beginning to imitate others' behavior. The basic unit of our society, the family, is built upon this kind of learning. In a good family situation children pick up many of the beliefs and values of their parents, even their mannerisms and tone of voice. Modeled learning also takes place in more specialized contexts. Think, for example, of the prophetic bands in the Old Testament, of Jesus' relationship with the Twelve, and of the group around Paul involved in his work. Unfortunately, modeled learning has been displaced in most Christian circles by the schooling or academic approach. Although the prophetic, discipling, and apostolic model was chiefly designed for people in long-term common work, it has and can still operate with people who come together more intermittently.

In certain respects this approach to learning is similar to that which goes under the name of "apprenticeship" or "discipleship" in some charismatic or conservative Christian circles. But both of these contain features which are either opposed to or absent from what I have in mind. For example, they tend to have an anti-intellectual and authoritarian element. For them, while learning the Bible is important, developing a more systematic understanding of how Christianity relates to life is not. While techniques of spiritual development, personal evangelism, and church growth are given attention, understanding of the wider social and cultural context is generally overlooked. While there is a close relationship between teacher and pupil, there is a tendency for leaders to reproduce others in their own likeness rather than enable them to find their own ministry. In any case, the "apprenticeship" model is rarely employed with Christians who are not proceeding to more church-related forms of ministry and the "discipleship" model concentrates more on the inner life and on evangelism than on a wider range of concerns.

Unfortunately, outside the family, where it is becoming increasingly narrowed anyway, there are few areas in secular life where modeling plays a significant part in the learning process. Until fairly recent times it was present in a number of occupations, such as nursing, but now these are also placing more emphasis upon formal rather than on-the-job training. In areas of life where overtones of the master-apprentice relationship remain, as in postgraduate supervision or in manual training, the relationship between the two tends to be rather circumscribed, even where both are Christians.

How then might modeled learning take place in connection with everyday life issues? Recently I took a number of people from my church cluster on a ten day visit to another city. This arose from an invitation to my wife and myself to help an inner-city congregation think through the pressures of time in everyday life, as well as related matters concerning lifestyle, relationships, and spirituality. Up to a few years ago I normally accepted such invitations and handled them alone. But now I always ask if I can bring a team with me. As a group we plan and prepare for such visits. We run them together, presenting our material in a variety of ways and in a variety of combinations. After we return home, we evaluate what we have done and talk about what we have gained from it. Frequently members of the team learn new things themselves and develop a greater coherence in their beliefs. They also discover new ways of communicating their beliefs and experience a greater confidence in sharing them.

Several days after our return from an earlier trip—involving ten days with a congregation and two days with a clergy group, focusing on ways of creating community in the local church—I was sufficiently struck by the effect of these visits upon those who came with us to write the following:

Earlier in the year Julie and I had wanted to run a course so that a number of people involved in our groups could deepen their understanding of the nature and role of the church. But we have not yet had the opportunity to do this, and we were not sure how to do it in a way that would be fresh and practical. We now realize that those who came with us to take part in the time with the congregation and clergy group had a theological learning experience of the most vital and profound kind. In both places, though at different levels, Julie and I were able to go through a wide range of material, presenting it in fresh ways and relating it to the situations of our hearers. The other members of the team were able to contribute in both settings — out of their knowledge and experience — and found that doing so clarified many things for them. They also found that observing and hearing us in action, at times in ways new to them, enabled both their understanding of the church and ability to talk about it to be enhanced. They have come home very excited about this. The experience has also enabled them to feel the power of what they believe and see its relevance to other churches. This suggests to us that, rather than thinking or running a course on the subject, we should seek to involve more people in such exercises so that they too can learn in the same holistic way.

Various aspects of everyday life could be handled in the same way. But this is also open for others, whose main ministry is through their paid employment or work at home. For example, if you have built up considerable experience of your occupation or profession as well as a biblical perspective upon it, you could give time to helping younger believers in the same line of work to develop a Christian framework for and approach to their job. This could be done relatively informally through inviting people into your own home, or where possible, through lunch hour discussions at or near to your work. There you could open up about some of the dilemmas, mistakes, and insights you have experienced and talk about common problems. More importantly you could build up a relationship with these people and exemplify the qualities they need to imitate. One of the contributing factors to the uncertainty that many younger Christians face in public life today is lack of adequate role models.[3]

A related way of helping people become more aware of certain everyday life issues is to design for them an "immersion experience," part of which involves exposure to a good role model at work. Such experiences are normally organized in connection with cross-cultural situations. A typical example would be a group of people from a congregation traveling to a Third World or Eastern European country to experience conditions and needs there first hand and discern what is an effective Christian response. But for many people in the church, including many pastors, conditions and needs in parts of a city or in certain workplaces are as unfamiliar and challenging. Churches or Christians in these settings could provide an immersion experience for such people and so generate thoughtful dialogue and reflection.

Becoming a Member of a Task Force

Several years ago I became involved with a small group of senior federal government workers who wished to develop a Christian perspective upon their work. We came together through the agency of a center committed to helping people in the work force relate their faith to their occupation. We met for a series of preliminary sessions, over breakfast or lunch, to work out how we wished to approach the exercises and what issues we wished to address. Out of this developed a working group consisting of five people who met over a three-and-a-half year period. Each member of the group, myself included, took responsibility for one major topic. I also spent time with each of them individually, assisting them to formulate a theological perspective on their chosen theme.

Throughout that period, we met monthly over an extended lunch hour or for an after work session so that all could share what they were doing. During those times we also worked our way through certain materials and issues relevant to the whole project. For example, we looked at a number of biblical figures who were involved in administration and at a number of other passages relevant to our concerns. We also examined writings by professional theologians and by people in the field of public administration that bore on the issues we were considering. Toward the end of our times together we also developed a number of case studies around the topics on which we were working.

Every nine months or so the working group presented its findings to a larger group of public servants. This in turn led to further research and discussion by the initial group. Some of the members made visits to other capital cities to enlarge their understanding of the factors involved at the state rather than federal level. At a later stage the group invited two others who had investigated adjacent areas of interest to contribute to its work. Finally, it organized a national conference of federal and state workers, augmented by representatives from other interested groups. Following this it produced a book containing all the major contributions, together with resource materials, in the hope that this would help other groups to form and wrestle with similar problems.[4]

This type of working group could be duplicated among members of many other occupations and professions. There are few fields of employment where Christians are engaged in such sustained reflection, despite the growing interest in the ethical dimensions of their faith. However, here and there groups are at work in similar ways. I know of some among economists, social workers, the media, psychologists, and accountants. Sometimes their concerns are less highly focused than in the group I have described, and not everyone accepts responsibility to investigate a particular issue. But they do attempt to address issues connected with their work in an ongoing, organized way.

A related approach to exploring industrial issues has been developed by the Department of Mission at Selly Oak College in Birmingham, England. This separates out the roles of facilitator and theological consultant and includes certain other ways of proceeding. The following are laid down to be followed:

1. The group itself rather than the resource person decides which of the issues raised by members will be investigated and agrees on a basic method of approach. The presenter of the situation-study then provides more detail, but remains silent till the group reconstructs it and "re-presents" it for checking. At any point in this process members may suggest a different direction or call attention to extra factors.

2. The group's "knowing," as established by their common work, now becomes the basis for what follows. While it can ask the presenter of the issue for more detail, at some point the members cannot ask for any more information. This matches the real life situation in which people often have to deal with problems involving inadequate information.

3. The main features of the development of the situation-study are elaborated on and listed on a board. This includes pinpointing the pressures falling on people, the major powers at work, and the human consequences. Then some search is made for one or two "handles" on the situation so that a practical way into the problem can be opened up.

4. The next step is to identify the policies being pursued by the principal parties, assess the world view and value judgments that underline these policies, and develop a theological critique of these views and values.

5. At this point it may be helpful to call in some theological

experts, who might also provide help with more general questions deserving attention that the group has unearthed.

6. From this point on there is a search for an alternative theological basis for dealing with the situation, a delineation of policies which might be developed from this basis, and the testing of such policies for realism, particularly by persons who will be involved in implementing them.

7. By now the group has developed a strong sense of community and members are in a position to offer personal support to any of their number who is having to cope with the situation.[5]

This working group approach is an effective way of exploring subjects other than professional or industrial matter. If you are a member of a special interest or single issue group, for example, in addition to any research and discussion you are already doing it is simply a matter of finding other Christians with the same concern who would be interested in developing a more explicit Christian understanding. More everyday, even routine activities could also be pursued in a similar way: all that you would need is a certain degree of shared experience, a willingness to stay with the group until the work is done, and access to a person who has some theological expertise combined with a sensitivity to everyday issues.

You might approach some of these matters by enrolling in a course of study or joining a study group, but for many issues you would find this less helpful. Few aspects of everyday life have been explored adequately from a Christian point of view for anyone to teach them effectively or prepare resource materials for study group use. In any case, a course of study can only give a second hand appreciation of the issues. It cannot really match the more concrete learning that takes place through belonging to a working group.

However, sometimes it is difficult to find other people to form a working group around a particular subject. In a particular congregation, place of employment, or special interest group, there may not be sufficient people with the same concerns or enough time. If this is the case, contacting a Christian resource center or lay education institute may put you in touch with others who have similar interests. If this fails to provide what you are looking for, or at the present you do not have the time to give to a working group, then a study group or course, if such exists, may have to do for the present.

The Power of Participatory Thinking

Over the last two decades the workshop has become a familiar part of the adult education scene. The difference between a working group and a workshop is partly a matter of numbers and partly a function of time. Whereas a working group normally involves only a few people, a workshop can encompass a larger number. A working group generally continues over a period of time, whereas a workshop is a briefer, more intensive affair.

Although workshops have been part of the Christian scene for a while, there is still a tendency to favor the seminar or conference as a context for learning. Even where workshops are available on a variety of topics, there seems to be little attempt to develop a pattern of integrated learning around them. Workshops are mostly isolated events. There is also an inclination to use workshops for less demanding subjects. For that reason many people feel, wrongly in my view, that they are not a suitable vehicle for dealing with complex issues.

Workshops certainly provide an excellent way of grappling with a wide range of practical dilemmas. As an example, consider the issue of busyness and the pressure of time. When I first began to be invited to speak on this subject I tended to tackle it alone in a highly instructional way. But increasingly I have moved in a more workshop direction and involve others with me as resource persons. We have found that a workshop on this topic is most effective when it takes place over an extended period of time; that is, intensively over a weekend or less intensively over a week or fortnight.

We attempt to find out at the very beginning where those attending it are in relation to the time issue. Each group is different and it is important for us to find out how they are affected by this pressure. One way of discovering this is to encourage everyone to engage in personal reflection for a period of time, writing down what comes to mind and then sharing it, if they wish, with the group as a whole. Once we have learned where members of the group are in relation to the time issue, we know whether we have to restructure what we have planned and give more attention to some matters than others.

Turning the whole group into a workshop also enables the participants to discover for themselves the main factors which quicken the pace of life and engender busyness. This also enables them to "own" their responsibility in the matter as well as "disown" factors over which they have no control. My role in that process is simply to ask the right kinds of questions and to group the responses in an instructive way, in this case distinguishing between the way our goals, values, drives, circumstances, and inadequacies affect our approach to time.

If the group has its attention drawn to the most important biblical passages dealing with time, it is able to begin developing its own Christian perspective on the problem. This is best done by dividing it into discussion groups and asking them to report their findings when they come back together. We have found that there is no need for directive questions about the passages for study. Groups unearth for themselves the basic principles which should affect their attitude to time and use of it. My contribution is then to order these and expand on them where it is helpful to do so.

At the close of the time, after we have shared some of the ways we have begun to overcome the pressures of time, we invite others to share with the whole group any helpful hints which they have discovered for themselves. This procedure tends to be less prescriptive and threatening as well as more practical and diverse than other ways of recommending a solution. Finally everyone is asked to spend some time quietly listing a few concrete steps they can take to reduce the degree of busyness in their lives. They are encouraged to resolve prayerfully with God to do something about these in the coming week.

I have gone into some detail here to convey a sense of the way in which any group of Christians with a modicum of help from a well-prepared resource person can workshop its way through to its own conclusions. As a learning experience this is far more effective than heavy doses of instruction from the front, even where this contains incisive sociological analysis, biblical exposition, and detailed application. This kind of instruction tends to evaporate soon after the session is over whereas what people have analyzed, worked out, and decided for themselves is much more likely to stay with them. It is far easier for the resource person to have a high profile and do almost everything up front. It is much harder to design such a workshop, discern when and how it must be varied while it is in process, and coordinate individual or group responses in a way that does most justice to them.

But the workshop approach is not only suited to practical matters. I have also used it extensively in apologetic work with small
groups of "doubters." We begin by hearing their stories about how
they came to their present views. The issues that emerge form
the "curriculum" of the remaining meetings as we deal with one
person's central doubt each week. This approach keeps these issues close to the everyday experiences which often generated
them, insuring that they are not discussed in a purely cerebral
way.

With respect to vocational ethics, workshops based upon case
studies are an excellent way of opening up problem areas. The
case study approach is widely used in management schools and
administrative training and is also being introduced into formal
theological education. One of the difficulties is that good case studies arise out of a long process themselves. They do not come
easily, even when built upon the experiences of those who are
formulating them, and it is the prior efforts of a working group that
often stands behind them.

The respected Christian educator Thomas Groome also empha-
sizes the value of workshops. He has tested these out on a wide
range of groups in a wide variety of settings. In his book *Christian
Religious Education,* he explains what he calls his "shared praxis"
approach:

> Over the past years I have used a shared praxis approach
> with adults and high school and grade school students (in
> both school and parish contexts), in weekend retreats, semi-
> nars, symposia, conventions, community renewal and team
> training programs, and so on. Gradually, from both apparent
> successes and failures, five recognizable pedagogical move-
> ments have emerged. . . .
>   i. the participants are invited to name their own activity
> concerning the topic for attention (present action);
>   ii. they are invited to reflect on why they do what they do,
> and what the likely or intended consequences of their action
> are (critical reflection);
>   iii. the educator presents to the group the Christian story
> concerning the topic at hand and the faith response it invites
> (story and its vision);
>   iv. the participants are invited to appropriate the story to

their lives in a dialogue with their own stories (dialectic between story and stories);

v. there is an opportunity to choose a personal faith response for the future (dialectic between vision and visions).

There is really nothing sacred about the number five, and other educators may find it helpful to adjust, combine or increase the movements.[6]

Workshops certainly could be used in many current learning contexts such as annual camps, houseparties, or conferences. Where they do take place in these settings, they tend to be on the margins not at the center of the program. One writer has said the following about what happens when experts and addresses dominate these gatherings:

All that is left to the whole body of people is to react, positively or negatively, to what has been presented to them. The more brilliant the speaker is, the less they are free to think their own thoughts and make their own contribution. The alternative is to replace keynote speakers with resource persons; and plan preparation to find out what, in their situation, participants are facing or should be facing. Agreed homework is then done in anticipation . . . it is those who have done this homework who are the catalysts. They share and check theological insights, working in small groups and then in plenary; identify pastoral responsibilities; commit themselves to forms of action; and, using their own words, draw into worship the longings, discoveries and rejoicings which had surfaced over the time of encounter. The specialist gives the people confidence that the work is properly theirs, helps the process to develop so that they make the most of what is theirs and of what is given them by others, and is ready to intervene to add some theological reflections or question some findings.[7]

As those of you who have been involved extensively in well-organized workshops know, the workshop approach to learning has many advantages. It engages us more fully than traditional modes of teaching so that we absorb more of what is being discussed. It develops our capacity to listen to and learn from one another and so brings out into the open the underlying perceptions and feelings that shape our attitudes. It draws on a wider range of insights and experience and therefore encourages both more subtle and more specific learning to take place.

The key to good workshops is a group that shares a common concern and at least one resource person willing to assist. Sometimes you will find such a group and person in a congregation or other Christian organization. Alternatively, a resource center or lay education institute may put you in touch with others who have similar concerns and with someone who can provide resources.

Several Heads Are Better Than One

Study groups which meet in a work environment or around a common concern also have their place. In the past, Christian occupational groups have tended to operate mainly for a devotional purpose or to provide fellowship for their members. Only rarely have such groups, or the annual conferences which sometimes bring their members together, focused on their work situation and the institutions to which they belong. During the last two decades study groups have begun to develop more around a range of moral and social issues. On some of these issues resources are available from denominational, parachurch, or secular groups. As yet, however, study groups have given less attention to more everyday matters and their dynamics sometimes hinder their members from working in a holistic way.

In his book *Working Out Your Own Beliefs: A Guide for Doing Your Own Theology*, Douglas Wingeier makes a number of useful suggestions which members of study groups wishing to develop a personal theology might employ, both in preparation for the group and when it meets. Preparing for the group may involve general reflection, focused meditation, and journal writing. He begins by proposing that you write down an important decision you made recently. This should include something about the background, alternative choices involved, and factors supporting or opposing these. Then add how you felt during or after the decision, what values you said yes or no to in deciding the way you did things, what God was trying to say to you through the process, and in what ways your decision is consistent with the biblical message, church teachings, your ideals, or previous experience of God's guidance.

He suggests various ways of building on this in the group meeting. For example, each person in the group could list the ten values they affirm most strongly or five goals they most wish to accomplish. Then everyone chooses the two values and goals that most guide their behavior, share these with someone whose values and goals are not too dissimilar and finally debrief as a group, voicing feelings, learnings, needs, and common goals. Focused prayers similar to those mentioned above could conclude the gathering. This exercise, he says, helps people to begin making the connection between faith and life.

Since he defines "doing theology" as "reflecting on experience from the stance of faith, making use of the resources of Scripture and Christian tradition," Wingeier then offers four pairs of exercises for private and group use, similar in style to the above, focusing in turn on learning from experience, reason, Scripture, and tradition. So in the next time of private preparation, we should concentrate on and write about an experience rather than a decision. The accompanying time of group reflection could center on sharing or discussing this. Alternatively, it could involve imaginatively entering into a biblical story and then talking about how it affected us, or choosing a biblical term that identifies something in us and asking what experience led us to use this and a simile we might prefer to put in its place, again sharing our reflections with the group.

In the following weeks individual preparation focuses on a key turning point in life, next a meaningful Bible passage, and finally a film, book, event, or Scripture. He suggests we seek to interpret these, identifying feelings and images associated with them, discerning the presence of God and responding to what is learned both practically and prayerfully. The corresponding group exercises involve:

1. portraying or diagramming a key turning point in our lives and allowing discussion to focus on the world view reflected in the story that explains it, the role of conscience in what takes place, and the self-image involved;

2. finding a particular character, parable, image, or event in the Bible with which we can identify and reflecting on the good news, encouragement, or challenge in the story;

3. selecting a central phrase from the creed, checking out

116 REDEEMING THE ROUTINES

its scriptural basis and traditional meaning and asking how far
it is a vital part of our own experience and shaping factor in
our lives.[8]

Wingeier's approach moves out from everyday experience and
draws on the Bible to correct and extend that. In my view the role
of the Bible could have been emphasized more. But it is also
possible to begin with the Bible first and move out into everyday
experience. In England, John Davies has developed a useful approach to Bible study that keeps it in touch with ordinary concerns. He describes this as follows:

> We take time off from our ordinary program of life; we pick
> up the Bible; we read a passage, say, which describes an
> event in the activity of Jesus. The first thing we must do, is
> to establish connections with our immediate experience. Rel-
> evant questions are:
> - What does the story connect with in our experience?
> - What bells does it ring in our memory?
> - What little details in the story interest us? Why?
> - Are there any problems for us in the story?
> - What character can we identify with?
> - Would we like to be the teller of the story? Why?
>
> Having read the event in its original context more thorough-
> ly, further questions can then be asked. For example:
> - Do we see anything interesting about the place which
>   the story has in the Gospel?
> - Why do we think the writer was interested in the story?
> - Why do we think that Christians in the early church
>   were interested in the story?
>
> Finally, the group turns back to the present. Relevant ques-
> tions now are:
> - What message or mandate do we get from the story:
>   for ourselves?
>   for our disciple group?
>   for our neighborhood?
>   for our country?
>   for the world?

- Who or what is being commended in the story in contemporary terms?
- Who or what is being criticized?
- What new attitudes are encouraged?
- What new action is suggested for the disciple-community today?[9]

Group members then go back to their ordinary program of life. This approach has some similarities with that developed by Walter Wink in the United States.

A further approach to Bible study is the so-called "narrative exegesis" one. Weaving biblical materials into a story rather than argument is a very fruitful way of bringing people into touch with what the Bible says. The story format enables them to enter more fully into and discover more fully for themselves what the Bible contains. Such a story triggers people's own stories about similar incidents, occasions, questions, and concerns and this enables a greater interaction to take place between God's revelation and our present situation. Both Walter Hollenweger and Hans Reudi-Weber have developed materials along this line, and my own *Going to Church in the First Century* is similar in character.[10]

Study groups require access to helpful resources if they are to work effectively. This may come through a member of the group. While such a person may have some familiarity with academic theology, this is not strictly necessary. Alternatively, discussion group material may be provided by an outside institution. In this case, all the group needs is a good facilitator. A competent facilitator is more important than a leader; that is, one who claims to know what is best for the group and controls its operation. The presence of a leader in this sense, or of an expert in theology, is more of a hindrance than a help unless this person is willing to have a low profile and act as a resource person.

The value of properly formed study groups is evident. Since they depend upon each member making a contribution, they increase the possibility of a better grasp of the matter they are discussing. They provide a context in which a variety of everyday issues can come up for inspection. But such groups function best when they are not just forums for exchanging ideas, but to some degree supportive fellowships as well. Only when this element is present will members feel free to talk about some of their significant interests and concerns. Where these groups take place in the actual environment in which the issue arises there is an extra edge to their deliberations.

Where Formal Learning Fits In

Where do formal courses of study fit into all this? There are two dangers to be avoided here. On the one hand, some people feel that gaining a Christian perspective on the routines of day-to-day living is incompatible with academic study. They would argue that turning it into a program of formal study takes it out of the everyday dimension and turns it into something more rarefied. But this only reinforces the view that the everyday dimension of life is secondary and not worth focused reflection. On the other hand, some people assume that developing a theology of ordinary life can only take place in an institutional setting through extensive programs of study. But full-time study in such a setting will only be possible for a small proportion of people. Also, formal study can only bridge the gap between belief and life at the level of thinking: it does not of itself ensure the right kind of character formation that empowers people to translate ideas into action.

Still, attending formal courses has some role to play in integrating belief and life. At some point in their lives, many Christians would benefit from the systematic thinking such study encourages. They will benefit most from this after they have had some experience in the world, so that they come to it having already formulated some questions and can test what they hear from the wisdom they have already accumulated. But what kind of content should such a program have? It should have a different starting point from the typical curriculum in a theological school.

An excellent example of what can be done is the interdisciplinary, team taught, faculty attended, Ministry of the Laity course at New College, Berkeley, California. Over a semester this class identifies all the main areas of life that require thoughtful Christian consideration and helps people to do this in a preliminary way. Areas covered include: *The vision: renewal in mind and life, Biblical studies for the laity, Historical and cross-cultural studies for the laity, Theological and ethical studies for the laity, Integrative studies and practical experience, Lay spirituality, Laity in the church, Lay people in society and culture, Laity in workplace and marketplace.*

Such a course opens up most of the relevant issues and lays a firm basis for any future study.

Before coming to the United States, we piloted two courses of study which give the average Christian a grasp of what is in the biblical writings and what is their Christian heritage. These courses, which run over a year each, are designed for groups of around eight people, including a facilitator. The first, the biblical overview, involves reading about twenty-five chapters of the Bible a week, keeping a daily summary of what is covered and meeting weekly for around two to three hours to share insights. This is not done with a view to gaining some systematic doctrinal or ethical understanding of what the Bible contains. Nor is it a guided tour in the sense that everyone is provided with set questions to which they must find answers from each set of readings.

There is a three-fold aim: (1) to help those taking part to gain an overall grasp of the biblical drama or story as part of the biography of God, (2) to trace a practical theme of their own choosing through the Bible, and (3) to be alert to points where God's story touches their own. The method is highly participatory: is an invitation to self-discovery and mutual sharing in which participants dwell on what strikes them from their readings—what excites them, puzzles them, troubles them, challenges them—rather than attempting to discuss every passage read or tie up every thread set loose. The enthusiasm generated by this way of approaching the Bible and its impact upon thinking and behavior has been nothing less than phenomenal.

We have followed this with a similar ten-month-long exercise introducing Christians to aspects of their "family tree." This Christian heritage course differs from conventional courses in church history in a number of ways. So far as the content is concerned, it focuses on key, life-giving movements and figures rather than endeavoring to give a blow-by-blow description of all that has happened. It looks not only at religious leaders and ecclesiastical developments, but at Christians who had a significant influence upon other areas of life such as social structures, law and injustice, science, politics, education, music and literature, family life, and spirituality. Throughout there is an eye to what these movements and figures have to say to us now in our twentieth-century situation. As far as method is concerned, once again each person reads material in preparation for the week's meeting. Each one also takes responsibility for investigating and presenting the life of four key figures throughout the year. There is a facilitator who has some general knowledge of the whole area or who has done the course already.

Both the biblical overview and Christian heritage courses train people, as they undertake them, to facilitate a group later themselves. Although not everyone will have the capacity to do this, each group should be able to produce one or two people who can do so. This means that the courses are self-reproducing and do not require the presence of an expert or theologically trained person within them. While recourse to such a person may be helpful from time to time, they are not needed on a week-by-week basis.

After completing the kinds of courses I have mentioned, if you wished to pursue further formal study, you might move in any one of a number of directions. In the biblical area, there could be a study of various everyday concerns — Jesus' attitude to such issues as work, leisure, morality, race, and politics. Sections of the biblical writings that especially impinge upon everyday life, such as the wisdom literature in the Old Testament and practical portions in the New, are also important. So far as history is concerned, attention could be given to the Christian interface with a particular aspect of intellectual, social, or cultural life. Some examples are: the contribution of "lay" theologians to a Christian understanding of society, the influence of Christian ideas and practice upon social welfare, and the development of modern music, painting, or literature from a Christian perspective.

In systematics, certain doctrines such as creation and providence, the kingdom of God, vocation, and the covenant are extremely relevant to everyday life issues. But then such central concerns as the incarnation, cross, resurrection, and eschatology also have significant implications in this area. I will say more about this in the final chapter. In drawing on the views of past Christian thinkers and leaders, a workshop approach can sometimes be extremely effective. Different members of the class can take the part of different sides to the debate as well as represent the views of contemporary religious groups who hold some of the same views. This enables them to get inside the positions adopted instead of looking at them from a distance.

With regard to ethics, there is a large range of questions you might explore: the ethics of sex, family, and the single life; moral, social, and political issues; profession and occupational concerns; our responsibility to the suburb, city, and the environment. It is possible to create an agenda around the particular ethical questions which people bring with them; indeed, these can provide the basis around which a whole course is run. Where other issues come up for consideration, far more can be gained from a case study approach than a conventional lecture format.

The more the formal courses of study are geared around the particular concerns which people bring with them, the more the traditional divisions between theological disciplines begin to fall away. It is questionable how far these govern appointments and courses in institutions oriented to the average Christian, for when a particular dilemma, interest, issue, or occupation is the chief focus of concern, we ought to bring every theological discipline to bear upon it. This means that interdisciplinary work will be the norm rather than the exception in any considered Christian approach to everyday life. So too will a new type of teacher, trained in some theological discipline perhaps, be more a skillful general practitioner than a specialist.

A Concluding Clarification

Throughout this chapter I have indicated the wide range of ways in which we can begin to redeem more effectively the routine pressures, situations, and responsibilities we encounter. At a number of points I have also emphasized the difference between these and conventional approaches to Christian and theological education. I would not wish to leave the impression that a theology by, for, and of the people is somehow less demanding than the other or inferior to it. John Macquarrie has stated the matter well:

> It cannot be asserted too strongly that lay theology is not, so to speak, theology made easy, a simplified or abridged version of a "professional" theology. Although in ordinary usage the word "lay" is often contrasted with "professional," it does not have that sense here. . . . A lay theology might well dispense with some of the jargon, though theology will always need some technical words for accuracy of expression. But a lay theology is not an easy version of an academic theology, and it would be an insult to the intelligence of the

layman to suggest that it is. All theology demands hard thinking. Lay theology is not a simplified version of academic theology but rather a corrective to it, broadening its base and bringing into being a theology that is more representative of the whole Christian community.[11]

If the theological education of ordinary Christians omits or only touches some parts of the traditional theological curriculum, it is because such items are less relevant, not because they are too difficult. The same rigor of thought that is required of those training for ordination — detailed attention to historical-critical methods, to the fine points of ecclesiastical doctrine, or to the subtleties of denominational relationships — must be applied to everyday life issues that concern the average Christian. These include the complexities of decision-making, the ambiguities of life in the public arena, and the distinctives of a genuinely Christian lifestyle. I am not suggesting that all Christians should reflect on such matters in the same way, to the same degree, or at the same level. But we must recognize that the dilemmas most Christians confront in *redeeming the routines* of everyday life are often as intricate, subtle, and perplexing as those that fill traditional theological textbooks.

Questions for Reflection:

1. Read paragraph one, page 100 starting, "But we do need. . . . " How should we decide which issues to concentrate on?
2. What advantages does the home church have for developing our theology? Read again pages 100 to 103.
3. In what ways is role modeling (pages 104 to 107) valuable?
4. What advantages does a working group (pages 107 to 109) have?
5. What makes a workshop (pages 110 to 114) work well?
6. Using Wingeier's suggestion of using an experience, not a decision, as a basis for theology (page 115), write down an experience and share and discuss it with your group along the lines suggested on pages 115 to 116.
7. Dilemmas for most Christians from everyday life are often as "intricate, subtle, and perplexing" as the issues that fill traditional theological textbooks. Share some issues that have arisen for you from being a Christian in the world.

FIVE
A People's Theology

If the first step in developing a Christian perspective on the routine aspects of life is finding an appropriate learning context, what happens next? By what means do we learn how to bridge the gap between biblical statements and the different, sometimes more complex situations we encounter today? How much can secular knowledge help us formulate a Christian response? Is there a distinctively Christian outlook on all everyday dilemmas? What is the role of those with formal theological qualifications in this process? Should certain matters have priority over others? In order to do justice of these issues, I will have to speak more specifically to professional theologians than I have done to this point.[1]

Every Person a Theologian

I believe a theology of everyday life works best when all Christians, not just professional theologians, are involved in it. Let us examine this under four main headings:

1. *Ordinary Christians can best identify their everyday concerns.*
I have already discussed my involvement with a working group of senior government workers. The members of this group were searching for ways in which they could bring their private values and public responsibilities into greater harmony. Our first task was to identify their dilemmas more precisely. Over the initial three-month period, meeting fortnightly, my task was simply to listen,

ask questions, and list the concerns they were expressing. At the end of this time, I helped them to categorize six main problem areas within which several types of difficulties arose. With this list in hand, there was further discussion about which matters should receive first consideration. This partly depended on what they saw as the most significant problems for them personally and what problems they felt they had most competence in tackling. From the list, four matters were eventually chosen as provisional topics.

This was not the end of the agenda-setting process. After members of the group had given preliminary consideration to these four topics, we arranged several further meetings with a wider range of public officials. It was up to this group to decide whether the four chosen problem areas provided the best starting point and whether they were being approached in the most fruitful way. Only at the end of this second series of meetings was it resolved to go ahead and explore the four issues in depth.

I learned far more from this stage of the process than I contributed. But for this to happen I had to leave behind certain attitudes programmed into me by my professional theological training. If you have had this training, you are tempted to think that you are the one to identify the issues which are important. In any case, professional theologians suffer from certain disadvantages in this whole area. The first has to do with the context in which most of them work. Bruce Wilson puts this well:

Perhaps the most significant change which the so-called process of secularization has brought to the modern church is the split in our consciousness, in our society, in our culture between the sacred and the secular. It is a split which enters into the life of our churches too. The laity, as we call them, live, and more importantly work, in that zone of occupation loosely called secular. The clergy, as we call them, live, work, and experience most of their face-to-face relationships in the zone of the sacred. And whatever we call them, academic theologians or lecturers in theology mostly live, work and have their being in academicized ecclesias or ecclesiased academies.[2]

In other words, the professional theologian and the average Christian do not, in many respects, inhabit the same mental world.

Though this is not true of all those who have undergone formal theological training, it is true of many such people. In most cases, theologians are ordained and work in ecclesiastical institutions. Their training and ethos set them at two removes from the majority of Christians. Of course, some theologians are not ordained and work in an academic setting. To some extent this enables them to escape what Bruce Wilson terms the "priestified theology" that often emerges from theological institutions. But these theologians frequently fall prey to an "academicized theology" that only relates to an educated elite.

If you are a professional theologian, you might well object that you do after all carry on part of your life outside the ecclesiastical or academic domain. Like everyone else you read a newspaper in the morning and put out the garbage at night. You raise a family, look after a home, wash the car, work in the garden, and play sports like everyone else. In any case, do not many of the same problems that arise in other professions and settings invade the church and university as well? All this is true, but two problems remain.

If you work in an ecclesiastical context, this will tend to color what you see as important and not. Theologians often reside in a kind of ecclesiastical compound, especially when they live and teach in the same environment, and this bears a little of the same relationship to the outside world as did mission compounds in foreign cities. I say "a little" because I do not want to press the analogy too far. But many people who are not professional theologians do comment on the artificial flavor of so much theological conversation.

In addition, professional theologians only have access to some of the everyday concerns other Christians have. There are many that still lie outside the theologian's experience and these can only be explored in the company of a wider group of people. While books can sometimes help you get some feeling for these concerns and the context in which they arise, these do not cover every situation either and are rarely a substitute for contact with people involved in the situation itself. This is why the gap between academic theology and everyday life cannot be closed by people who live much of the time on the "sacred" side of the line determining what lies on the "secular" side. On their own such people can only guess what lies across the border.

2. *Ordinary Christians already have some elements of an everyday theology.*

Over the last few years I have had intermittent contact with a group of Christian economists. The group is a diverse one, with a mixture of people from the business world, university circles, and government administration. The group has been in existence a number of years. It meets every six weeks or so in the office of one of its members. While some group discussions center on books or articles recommended by one of the members or on a talk given by someone from outside, others stem from papers prepared by one of those present. Some of these papers have been collected and made available for distribution. The group has even arranged a small conference which drew together economists from two other cities.

At one point I was asked to give a theological response to a paper that had been discussed at the previous meeting. Its presenter, who worked in a government department, was challenging the existing economic model that guided government farming policy. The paper questioned a number of widespread economic assumptions, raised the question of values in a provocative way, and argued for the relevance of a religiously based social vision to policy formation.

I opened my remarks by saying that I was not going to give a theological response to the paper so much as make explicit the theological dimension that already existed in it, as well as elaborating on this by reference to insights from biblical and ethical studies. It was obvious that the integrity with which the presenter had been wrestling with rural policy in his work and the experience he had gained over many years as a working economist had enabled him to develop a thoughtful and fundamentally Christian approach to this area. Though he was not aware of many biblical and professional theological resources that might bear on the issue, he did have an intuitive feeling for them. In this way he was becoming what I like to term a de facto theologian with respect to his vocation.

I have to stress this in the face of another temptation for professional theologians. For even if they acknowledge the role of other Christians in drawing up an agenda of everyday concerns, they might assume that they are the ones to formulate the theological response to those concerns. Such theologians sometimes betray their attitude here by speaking about the importance of fashioning a theology *for,* and perhaps even *of,* the people of God, without recognizing that this must be a theology *by* the people of God as well. At this point a paternalistic note can all too easily insert itself. Professional theologians also display a paternalistic attitude when they think instinctively of providing courses on matters arising out of the ongoing business of life. In so doing they reveal their belief that they have or can find the answers to the questions the average Christian is asking.

This outlook is at odds with the authentic spirit of Christianity. While certain people undoubtedly have a responsibility to draw out the implications of the Gospel in a more subtle and systematic way than others, all Christians are capable of doing this in some measure, and in some areas only they can do this. As the Australian theologian Graham Hughes writes:

This is to suggest that there will be infinite gradation in levels of discernment at which the task of theology will be carried out. The man who sits down in his farmhouse kitchen with an open Bible, the educated housewife preparing to lead a senior Bible class group, the minister in his study or the professor in his library are obviously all working at very different levels and with very different audiences in view. What I want to say is that there is no essential difference in *what* they are doing, provided they are properly about their job. They are all trying to understand what God is saying to us today. They are all busy about the task of theology.[3]

Theology, therefore, is not only an academic subject for brighter Christians or for those who wish to become ordained.

We need to go further. Even Graham Hughes' examples of ordinary people doing theology are too oriented to forms of learning that involve study. What, for example, about learning that comes through insight? This kind of learning is not so much something we give ourselves to as something which is given to us. It is born out of attending to God in meditation and prayer. It is born out of attending to the created order and intuiting messages from it. It is born out of attending to life and receiving parables from it. Attentive waiting, wonder, and listening are the midwife of insight. And when insight is set beside insight, and there is an attempt to interpret and connect them, theology is in the making.

Learning also comes through careful observation. The processes of nature, its patterns and rhythms, can teach us a great deal about the character of God and the nature of everyday life. Other people's behavior can instruct us in a whole range of ways about how to behave or not behave; what is caused by and flows from certain kinds of actions; and which choices, possibilities, and alternatives exist when we have to make decisions. Observing these leads to understanding of a different kind of insight. One is deductive, the other inductive. One is won, the other given. Yet both have their source in God. Both these ways of learning can affect us unconsciously. But when we become aware of them and reflect on them, we are engaging in theological understanding.

Learning also takes place through personal experience.[4] It is not only as we study the Bible, hear a sermon, or read a religious book that we grow in Christian understanding; nor only as we observe the way others, structures, and nature work. Anyone who is reflecting Christianly in a serious and ordered way about their paid employment, child raising, or favorite sport is in the business of doing theology. In the examples I have given, such people are attempting to fashion from their experience a theology of vocation, marriage, and leisure respectively, in the hope that it will guide their daily living. Not that this is always a highly rational and systematic affair or something that only revolves around problems and decisions. Much of it flows spontaneously from the kind of person each is becoming and relates to any aspect of what each is engaged in.

Since many Christians are learning in all these ways, we should take encouragement from it. For it means that the general absence of a Christian understanding of everyday life at the public level does not mean it is altogether absent in the private sphere. In many instances the starting points and some of the directions are already there. The problem is that they have not been recognized as such or articulated enough. The first task is to bring to the surface those intentions, motives, dispositions, and principles which already guide the attitudes and actions of the kinds of Christians I have mentioned. Many of these starting points and directions may have inadequacies. Some may need to be discarded. Most will need to be developed. Most benefit from evaluation from appropriate people outside the setting in which they were developed. All will require scrutiny in the light of Bible teaching. But they are the basic building blocks of any theology of everyday life, and it is with them that we must begin.

3. *Everyday theology is a cooperative effort between ordinary Christians and professional theologians.*
A few years ago, in preparing to write a book on the tyranny of time in modern life, I learned much from a broad range of people about the difficulties they had with time and the questions these provoked. I also learned that some individuals, families, and groups had discovered ways of coping with the problem of time or creatively dealing with it. Only as I worked through the material with these and other groups was I able to gain further insight into the problem. I made it my business to raise the matter in conversation whenever I had opportunity to do so. I regularly sought out occasions where I could share what I was thinking in greater depth. I was able to do this in a variety of contexts: day seminars, weekend conferences, week-long units and semester courses; and with audiences as diverse as students, teachers, public officials, politicians, and missionaries, as well as many heterogeneous groups of Christians.

I gained a great deal from these discussions. Some of the comments made opened up new perspectives which I had not thought about. Some of the ideas I advocated were challenged. Several times I was provided with practical recommendations for dealing with the pressures of time. As a result of encouraging people to respond to these sessions in other than purely verbal ways, I was offered songs, hymns, stories, parables, cartoons, and prayers which crystalized people's feelings about our wrestling with the issue. In many respects, then, my work on the problem of time and the book which came out of it was a corporate effort, a mosaic of contributions from a wide range of Christians. Whatever value it has owes much to this.

If as a professional theologian, you wish to deal with the routines of everyday life, you cannot simply sit down in your study and — with the help of biblical, theological, and other relevant writings — provide what is needed. You must involve a wide range of Christians in the process. They are not simply there to frame the questions and suggest some of the ingredients. They have a fundamental role to play in developing both the theoretical and practical understanding of the issue. This is even more clearly the case when the matter under discussion is not one with which you are familiar but distinctive to their own situation. There are two steps to consider here.

First, those who have had direct exposure to the issue at hand have a greater understanding of the situation. Others may look in from the outside and discern something of what is involved. Because of their detachment they may even see certain things more clearly. But those who are closest to the heart of any issue do have access to all kinds of information — technical, practical, and perhaps even theoretical — which is essential to any informed response. Admittedly, some of this information can be gleaned from reports and statistics, from academic studies, and from fictional accounts of similar situations. But it is rare for these sources to provide the sharp definition of an issue that comes from someone on the scene. Nothing compares to an expert. As German theologian Jürgen Moltmann is fond of saying to theological students in his courses on Christian Ethics: when a doctrinal dispute emerges in the church, you are the experts. But when an ethical dilemma arises in secular life, it is Christians touched by it who are the experts, not you. In such matters, you are not the professionals and they the laypeople; you are the laypeople and they the professionals.

Second, Christians who have some stake in the issue under discussion are able to interpret theologically the information they have to bring to it. It is through the give and take of discussion that the most significant factors for an issue become apparent. It is by the same means that a Christian perspective on it comes into sharper focus, each helping the other to go beyond the de facto theological insights they already possess. This takes time, for understanding in depth rarely comes quickly. It takes even longer to work out effective recommendations for action. It is at this point that so many reports or statements emanating from church bodies are at their weakest. Such bodies tend to have too many "experts" and not enough grass-roots representatives. Without the participation of a wide variety of people — from all kinds of class and ethnic backgrounds, with all types of educational and practical qualifications, and in all sorts of work and non-work situations — a fully-rounded and thoroughly relevant theology of everyday life will not come into existence.

4. *A workable theology of everyday life requires practical testing by ordinary Christians.*
Over many years those involved in the house churches with whom we have had contact have felt that they would like to share their experiences with a wider audience. In the first instance, this centered on talking about what we had discovered with interested congregations and parachurch organizations. But there was also the thought that at some time it would be appropriate for us to put our thoughts on paper. Now and again we were encouraged by a publisher to do this. But for a long time neither we nor others in our groups felt that we had learned enough to do this.

Consequently, apart from two or three general articles, it was more than fifteen years after our groups had begun that the moment to write something substantial seemed right. To have written anything on the subject before that would have been premature. Not that we felt when the moment came that we had fully "arrived"—far from it. But at least the model had been tested sufficiently to put it before others with some confidence. The book that resulted was in large measure a communal exercise, gathering together the contributions of people in a variety of house churches, jointly edited and written by my wife and myself. Only so, we felt, would the book capture some of the real flavor and diversity of home church life.[5]

Unfortunately thinking and learning in the West tend to take place chiefly *for* rather than *through* practice. Theory comes first and application follows. We learn now in order to act later. In this way we separate, at times even invert, processes that are commonplace in other cultures. Undoubtedly, our approach has many virtues: our extraordinary scientific and technological development bears witness to that. But it has also generated problems for which we do not as yet have answers. In fact, our impotence partly stems from the way we bring the very same faculties to bear on remedying problems that created those situations in the first place. We persist in thinking that we can always work out solutions in the abstract instead of realizing that they will only emerge as thought and acting interact and modify one another.

Christian thinking over the last few centuries has largely succumbed to this approach. In this matter we have been more shaped by our culture than we realize. We also tend to concentrate on learning *for* rather than *through* action. From Sunday School lessons, through Bible study groups, and into theological education our minds are filled with information for future use. While some of this is valuable, even necessary, too much of it creates a dangerous divorce between thought and behavior, doctrine and life. For our most significant learning takes place through a subtler yet more practical process. It takes place through the constant interplay of reflection and action, each oriented toward the other. While there is a place for more general instruction that is not closely related to behavior, this is secondary. I do not wish to devalue its importance, but it is not what changes people or society. As someone has said, "the problem with most Christian pedagogy (sermons, theological lectures, etc.) is that its primary purpose is *information* rather than *transformation*."[6]

Yet the Bible endorses the more dynamic approach to learning and the lives of many major Christian pioneers and thinkers illustrate it. The meaning of the word *know* in the Bible, often commented upon by theologians but rarely influencing the way they teach, binds understanding and doing inextricably together. To "know" is not merely to understand what God has said, nor is it to do what you understand. For you only show that you understand by doing and it is in the doing that understanding partly comes.

Paul exemplifies this: his profound theological insights did not come to him overnight, nor did they drop out of the blue. It was mainly through coming to terms with personal suffering and social humiliation, and through engaging with problems his congregations were encountering, that his understanding developed. In large measure this was also true of such people as Augustine, Luther, and Calvin. Attention recently has been given to the centrality of the idea of "relevance" in Calvin's writings, and it was this that gave the consistently practical cast to the best of Puritan preaching and writing. If any group of Christians took seriously the importance of relating their systematic beliefs to all the routines of life it was the Puritans. While the more extreme oppressive effects of some of this have lingered long in Western consciousness, any close reading of the leading Puritans demonstrates how much concern there was to relate theology to everyday concerns in a vital and balanced way. Wesley continued this tradition as did several of the earliest evangelicals such as Wilberforce, who himself wrote on the need for what he termed "a reformation of manners." Significant strands in the thought of such figures as Kierkegaard and Bonhoeffer also possess this character. In all these people thinking and acting shaped and informed one another. Reflection was directed toward life and was also influenced by it. This is why so much of what they wrote remains vital and relevant today.

A Christian understanding of *redeeming the routines* of life must possess something of the same spirit. If it is forged into the warp and woof of everyday life it will also have vitality and relevance. The best person to implement and judge the value of any Christian approach to everyday situations is the average Christian. But it takes time to do this and the process must not be hurried. If it is short-circuited through the desire for quick results, whatever comes out of it will not be adequate. Only if it is given its proper time will the real benefits appear. Whatever emerges will then have a sharper cutting edge and become a genuine force for change.

If a Christian theology of everyday life allows its agenda to arise from the concrete dilemmas that ordinary people confront, if it builds on the best features of the rudimentary theology that some Christians have already developed, if it arises from discussion involving a wide range of people wrestling with a common problem, and if it is also tested by such people for its practical value, it will have much to offer.

A Theology of the Whole Person

1. Toward a Holistic Approach to Life

I would not wish to give the impression that developing a Christian approach to all the routines of life only involves serious thought or detailed recommendations. We are constantly in danger of overstressing the role of the intellect in our lives. We are also vulnerable to developing casuistic regulations to guide our behavior. If we succumb to the first danger, we have fallen into the Greek temptation that Paul inveighs so strongly against in his letters to the Corinthians. If we succumb to the second, we have fallen into the Pharisaic temptation that Jesus attacked so consistently throughout His ministry.

First, we are more than thinking machines. There is a rationality of the emotions, imagination, and will as much as of the intellect. Only when we are developing in *all* these areas will we live

fully integrated Christian lives. Only as we are becoming mature in
our feelings and intuitions, discovering the most powerful and penetrating images for viewing reality, and strengthening our ability to
commit ourselves to difficult courses of action will we become and
do what we want. Relying on the rationality of our intellects alone
will not take us far enough.

For example, our basic thinking is done through images not
propositions, though propositions flow from these images, and only
if our imaginations are being renewed will our thinking follow suit.
As Richard Boholm says, "Many of the values and beliefs we hold
are expressed through images and . . . these images largely govern
our behavior. To change one's behavior involves changing the
images that instruct and reinforce that behavior. . . . "[7] That is why
the Bible speaks to us so often through images — God as a father,
Christ's death as a sacrifice, the church as a body, the Christian
life as a walk, heaven as a city.

Similarly, unless our emotions are being trained alongside our
intellects, then our lives will not reflect the passionate, deeply felt
side of God revealed to us in the prophetic and apostolic writings,
but only His thoughts. We will think and act like computers, lacking not just the feelings to go with our attitudes, but the sensitivity which helps us discern what is appropriate behavior anyway.
And what use would it be to know how to think about and negotiate everyday life if we did not have the power to live that out? In
itself, broadening and deepening our understanding does not necessarily lead to changes in our behavior, and unless we are becoming more empowered as well as more knowledgable we are not
changing in any fundamental way.

This means assisting Christians to develop the right kind of
character as well as the right kinds of ideas. If all a theology for
everyday life produces is a series of principles and recommendations, it will have fallen into the same trap as the casuistic books
on ethics written for earlier generations of Roman Catholics and
Protestants. Such principles and recommendations have their
place. But as well we need potent images, symbols, and models to
stimulate our thinking and behavior. We also need freedom and
flexibility to intuit what we should do in situations which are untypical or in which more than one option is valid. We do not always
need to have detailed regulations at hand in order to live
responsibly.

There is another problem with the casuistic approach to life. Practical though some of the older manuals were, often they lacked vitality. They did not give life so much as constrain it. They failed to realize that our actions are fundamentally a function of our character. I am not suggesting that if only we attend to forming character we will automatically do what is right. That would be the opposite, pietistic error. Our character develops as we become increasingly aware of the complexity of life and wrestle with specific decisions we have to make. It also develops as we connect up the various parts of our lives into an integrated whole and have some sense of where we have come from, where we are now, and where we are heading. Having a sense of our own "story" and gaining a feeling for others' "stories" is also necessary if we are to act rightly.

Most basic of all is a real familiarity with God's "story" as revealed in the Bible. The Bible is only secondarily a source of doctrine and ethics, of beliefs and principles; primarily it is "the greatest story ever told" and as such it has the profoundest impact upon the individual "stories" we write for our own lives, right down to the most everyday level.[8]

2. Developing a Down-to-Earth Spirituality

If character plays a vital part in our ability to act Christianly in everyday situations, we cannot overlook the importance of those contexts which most helpfully shape it. Here I can only stress the central—and mutually dependent—place that both relating to God and relating to others must have in our lives. Unless I am clearing time for God to show Himself to me and love me, to reveal His dreams for me and deepen my affection for Him, to talk to and with me, and to empower me through the wide range of ways He makes His Spirit available to me, I will never get very far in developing an integrated Christian life. And unless I am in a real relationship with a small group of fellow Christians, opening myself up to them and learning how to love them, sharing my dreams with them and growing in sensitivity to them, reflecting on what God is saying and open to their correcting, I will only get so far but no further. In fact, so dependent are these two ways of relating on one another, that I cannot even get very far with either one unless I am deeply involved in both. This is as true for the professional theologian as for anyone else.

But both relating to God and relating to others — piety and community — must be inextricably intertwined with the everyday world
in which we live and not escape from it or haven in it. Our
spirituality should not only touch our so-called inner life — which in
any case is significantly shaped by all that we do and experience in
our day-to-day affairs — but emerge through and connect with the
complex web of situations, incidents, and encounters that make up
our lives. It too should have an everyday cast to it: we should
constantly be meeting God *in* it, not only *apart* from it. Through
intimations, parables, and dreams as well as through what we hear,
read, and observe, the voice of God, which the psalmist reminds us
is never silent (Ps. 50:3), should echo in our minds.

In the midst of our daily activities, whatever they happen to be,
we should find reverberations of eternity — of the kingdom of God,
of the qualities, ethos, and values of heavenly life — coming to us.
These do not necessarily involve what is known, after Brother
Lawrence, as intentional "practice of the presence of God."[9] We do
not have to find ways of freeing up our minds and spirits for
meditation as we go about our everyday tasks. It is possible and
valid to do that when washing the dishes, sweeping the floor,
sitting in a bus, or even driving along a (relatively deserted) free-
way. But this is not the only way in which we can maintain an
ongoing direct connection between ourselves and God in the
course of even the most routine tasks.

For it is in the midst of even the most highly focused activity —
when all our mental, physical, or emotional energies are called
upon — that contemplative moments can occur. They occur in and
through the activity in which we are engaged, sometimes precisely
at the moment of the most intense involvement in it. The precon-
dition for such glimpses into the divine life is not abstraction from
the tasks at hand but genuine attentiveness to what is immediately
at hand. This enables us to not only see, feel, and hear it, but at
the same time to see and hear through it to the even more fundamental reality underlying it. Such sacramental moments can happen in the home, at work, or out in the open. They can take place
as much in a crowd as on our own.

I have already said something about Parker Palmer's approach
to spirituality along these lines.[10] Others come to a similar conclusion by talking about family life not just as a context for exercising
the spiritual disciplines but as a spiritual discipline itself.[11] This is

true, for family life generally shapes the quality of a person spiritually *more* than almost anything else. It is not just what takes place during the "quiet time" which is determinative here, but how one responds to the still, small voice of God and the quiet shaping work of the Spirit in and through the ordinary demands of the home. Much of the same can be said of friendship, another spiritual discipline as writers from Augustine through Jeremy Taylor to C.S. Lewis, have acknowledged.

This being the case, it is not difficult to see why the same is also true for work. Work in itself is—or can be—a spiritual discipline. Where it is intentionally approached in this way, it becomes not the antithesis of time apart with God but a time when God can be known and experienced. The phrase "a spirituality of work" is becoming more familiar in writings on both work and spirituality.[12] There is a good biblical foundation for this, for example, in the lives of such marketplace believers as Joseph, Nehemiah, and Esther. According to Paul, the quality of the work a person has done outside church in managing their household—which in biblical times was the place where work was done as well as the family raised—qualifies them to undertake a responsible role in the church (1 Tim. 3:5).

Our communal life with other Christians should also have its feet on the ground. Gathering with them ought not revolve around so-called spiritual concerns alone, but embrace every aspect of our lives. It is as whole people that we must relate to one another and church ought to be the place we show any of our concerns—in the home, at work, to do with our leisure, within our neighborhood, relating to our society at large. These are the matters with which the Scriptures should be brought into contact and which should become the subject of prayer, whatever else might be important for us to share with God and one another.

3. Integrating Doctrine and Ethics
Some of you might wonder whether the high profile I have given to ethical and other practical concerns is due to my devaluing the importance of doctrine. This is not so. What I am arguing for is the reconciliation of ethics and doctrine. They have been divorced too long and the separation is unbiblical. In the legal and prophetic writings in the Old Testament and in the teaching of Jesus and Paul in the New, doctrine and ethics are a seamless whole.

In fact, one could argue that what we call ethics predominates.[13] One is never discussed for long without reference to the other. It is we who have divided them and placed them in different compartments. This gap between doctrine and ethics is one of the reasons that we have failed to develop a satisfactory theology of everyday life. All key doctrines have their practical dimension just as all practical matters have their doctrinal aspect.

This being the case, we can only tackle many everyday issues by investigating basic Christian doctrines more deeply. For example:

• The doctrine of *creation* speaks to us of the dynamic activity of God in the world. It does so not only in general terms, but talks specifically about the quality of God's creative work and His concern for detail. The Bible establishes a connection between God's creativity and ours and between His work and our work. It alerts us to the need for a balance between work and rest as well as between production and appreciation. It affirms our trusteeship for the environment and our mandate to develop it responsibly. Creation also embraces the role of and our relationship with the animal kingdom.

• One of the most neglected doctrines is that of *providence*. If it does come into discussion, it is mostly in connection with God's general supervision of history or with the problem of suffering and evil. But the main theme of this teaching is His preservation of, care for, and involvement in the human, animal, and material world, at the structural as well as individual level. We can only make sense of many of our more everyday activities, ranging from routine matters like housework to interests like gardening or keeping pets, along with much of the voluntary and paid work that we do, if we view it within the framework of God's providence.

• The whole business of life, not just what happens in our individual family or church affairs, is the forum for working out our Christian responsibility.

■ In the past, Protestants developed a doctrine of *vocation* to express this conviction. This affirms all Christians as ministers of Christ, not only in the church but in the world, an idea that must be broadened to include other responsibilities like raising a family and other activities such as those we now refer to as avocations.

■ Those inclined in a more Roman Catholic direction placed greater emphasis upon the *incarnation*. This underlines our need to take the world seriously and not downgrade its importance and the importance of full identification with those in it, particularly with those who are disadvantaged in any way.

■ In the present more emphasis has been laid on the idea of *liberation.* Here we are reminded of the possibility of change in social, economic, and political structures as well as personal life.

All these have some part to play in developing a theology of everyday life, but there is an even more fundamental place for the central doctrines of the *cross and resurrection* of Christ. While these may seem somewhat removed from the realities of the workplace or of everyday routine, in fact they are not. The cross and resurrection remind us of God's inversion of this world's values and of the way in which this should influence our motives, choices, and behavior. There is a direct line between these central realities of the Christian faith and notions of servant leadership or transformation of the ordinary. And we should not forget the cosmic relevance of the cross and resurrection: their hidden impact upon the whole created and supernatural order.[14]

• *Justification* is one of the central biblical doctrines. In the past this has been upheld against attempts to circumvent it by a false emphasis on justification by works. Sometimes these works have taken the form of moral regulations, as with the Pharisees in the time of Jesus, or of ritual obligations, as with many Roman Catholics in the time of Luther. But nowadays people tend to justify their lives—whether to others, themselves, or God—primarily through their secular work or job. This is the main form that justification by works takes today and it is present within the church as well as outside it, even within the ordained ministry. The idolatry of work in modern life can only be dealt a mortal blow by means of a redirected doctrine of justification by faith.

• In fact, there is a vital place for a proper understanding of *idolatry* and of the role of the *principalities and powers.* With few exceptions there has been a singular lack of application of the idea of idolatry in Christian analyses of contemporary life. This is less true of the biblical teaching on principalities and powers, though often these have simply been identified with ideologies and social structures. We cannot understand the power, both constructive and destructive, of the pressures, traditions, institutions, and preoccupations in our society without looking at them through these biblical categories.

• The idea of the *covenant* is significant in thinking about our responsibility and accountability to others. This has reference to a number of areas in life. It is relevant to the work situation, especially with respect to promises, obligations, and contracts. In the spheres of friendship and marriage it provides the basis and informs the character of the relationships entered into. In regard to society at large the notion of covenant plays a central part in the formation and dynamics of voluntary associations.

• A fully developed theology of the *Holy Spirit* should recognize the rich potential and extraordinary diversity of the capacities God has given us. It would speak of the abilities given to people through the general activity of the Spirit in the world and with the Spirit's special presence in the church. The nature and exercise of power are also illumined through study of the Spirit's character and ways of operating. The significance of the group as a context for exercising any type of gift is also important.

• An appreciation of *eschatology* is also fundamental. This may seem surprising, for do not everyday concerns by definition have to do with this life and not the next? But we cannot separate the two, as Paul for one reminds us forcibly in 1 Corinthians 7:29-31. Everyday situations and responsibilities must be lived in the light of the eternal dimension; the quality of life in the latter throws light upon the norms that should characterize life in this world; the presence of hope and willingness to take the long-term view are also firmly rooted in our awareness and experience of heavenly realities.

It is not easy to translate such doctrinal convictions into practical recommendations. We can only do this if we take some intermediate steps which bridge the gap between the biblical world and our own. What form should those intermediate steps take? Some encourage us to frame "moral presumptions," which are what we might call the ethical "bottom line" from which our thinking should begin and the ethical "outer boundary" beyond which we cannot go. While no simple deductions can be made from these as to what we should do, they create room for a range of valid, changing, and even conflicting possibilities for action. Others talk about the need for "action-oriented principles," which are immediate implications of biblical principles that can be put into practical effect without further modification. These are applicable to any age, though general in character and requiring more detail to provide concrete guidance.

Still others favor the use of "operative norms." These are more specific, vary from one age or culture to another, yet still fall short of detailed policies or plans. Not all Christians are likely to agree to these. Finally, there are those who refer to the value of "middle axioms." These seek to maintain the highest level of agreement between Christians from a number of viewpoints while allowing them to be implemented in a variety of ways. To some extent these approaches are complementary, to some extent they are alternatives. I do not wish to evaluate them here, but simply emphasize the need for some kind of intermediate steps if we are to produce a biblically based but practically relevant Christian understanding of everyday life.

4. The Value and Limits of Specialist Resources

Where do specialist theological resources come in and who should be the one to investigate them? Let me discuss the resources first. Naturally you will want to draw on any biblical and theological studies that are relevant, but you will probably find that such studies are limited in value. The works of biblical scholars are useful for identifying many of the biblical passages relevant to everyday concerns, for giving the meaning of key images and concepts, and for providing signposts suggesting the general direction from which solutions may come. Newer socio-historical and sociological approaches to the Bible are valuable where they yield a clearer understanding of everyday life in biblical times, making it easier to discern the differences and similarities with our situation today.

But both older and newer style biblical studies rarely take up contemporary issues and, even where they do, tend to do this only in a general way. They also pay less attention to some materials that may be relevant to such issues. So when dealing with an everyday concern someone will have extra biblical work to do and will also have to work harder at applying it to the matter at hand. Whoever does this will find it rewarding to dwell on the wisdom materials in both the Old and New Testament. This material is often closest to many of the concerns of the average Christian. Its neglect is one of the reasons for the gap between belief and daily

life. Although we must not consider the wisdom writings indepen-
dently of other parts of the Bible, such as the prophetic writings
and apostolic letters, they are often a helpful starting point for the
consideration of everyday concerns.

I have found the work of systematic theologians to be as much
frustrating as helpful. Once it ranges beyond central doctrinal concerns which, though they often could be, are not frequently linked
to everyday issues, it tends to concentrate on philosophical or
perhaps broader social or cultural issues. The latter can be quite
interesting and at times form a background to the consideration of
more everyday concerns. But in my experience it is only now and
again, and generally in the writings of the leading theologians, that
everyday concerns occasionally come into view. The writings of
the great Danish thinker of the last century, Sören Kierkegaard, or
of Karl Barth, the most famous theologian of this century, contain
some marvelous flashes of insight into everyday problems.

Writings in Christian ethics are also helpful for the suggestions
they make about the best methods of approach and for the light
they throw on some current ethical dilemmas. But with some fine
exceptions, they tend to set out the biblical perspective on first-
century issues without dealing with their contemporary application
or deal with a limited number of contemporary issues without
doing justice to the biblical data. Increasingly, there seems to be a
concern to bring the Bible and contemporary problems together,
but there is still a long way to go. And such writings mainly focus
on problems, overlooking other aspects of life which are less problems than just part and parcel of life.

In dealing with issues of everyday life it is important to consult
materials from a wide range of other disciplines, such as history,
literature, psychology, economics, and sociology, as well as from
such areas as urban, media, managerial, and administrative studies. Whenever these are likely to throw light on the issue under
discussion, they should be investigated. So too should more wide-
ranging works on the history of ideas or behavior along with informed analyses of present cultural attitudes, forces, and trends.
As well as providing valuable information about the world in which
we live, these works at times contain pointers to or expressions of
God's truth. That is, they have picked up traces of His general
revelation. Too much theological reflection depends upon the Bible
or "special revelation" alone and does not take sufficient account

of other sources of knowledge. That is why it often seems remote from ordinary life. It is essential to test material from these other sources for false presuppositions, data, and interpretations, and to see how much or little of it is consonant with a biblical framework. But to overlook it is to miss some of the clues God has left lying about for solving the puzzles that daily confront us.[15]

Also not to be overlooked are popular or semi-popular writings which dissect a slice of contemporary life, synthesize insights from diverse academic fields, or present an individual response to our current way of life. Some of these do not have a great deal of sophistication, but at times they are more down-to-earth and perceptive than weightier discussions. Also relevant are non-literary areas such as popular music, contemporary film, and newspaper cartoons. Our reading should also embrace popular Christian writings. Now and again these show more insight than scholar's learned treatises. Sometimes the "foolishness" of those with less formal theological education is wiser than the "wisdom" of their more professionally qualified counterparts.

5. A New Paradigm for Theology

Who should have the responsibility of drawing in the specialized resources I have mentioned? Someone who has some formal training in theology would find it easiest to discover what is available and make most sense of it—but only if certain other factors are present. For example, such a person must be familiar not only with theological resources but with other specialized resources as well, otherwise there will be too narrow a perspective. It would be possible for someone else to identify non-theological resources that were available. This would present no problem so long as the two specialists could work together fruitfully. This points up the need for a quite different capacity.

The professional theologian must have some relational as well as intellectual skills. Otherwise there will be no genuine cooperation even with other specialists, quite apart from other Christians involved in the process. In fact, the professional theologian must be prepared to be a servant to others in the group. This is another area where the notion of "servant" or "enabling" leadership must be present. If the professional assumes control over the group or allows specialized resources to overwhelm the empirical experience others bring to it, very little of worth will emerge.

You will contribute most to such an exercise if you are seeking to develop a theological perspective on your own daily activities. It is easier to integrate your thinking and actions at this point than in areas of life with which you are less familiar. This was so for me with respect to the issue of time. It had arisen as a personal problem long before I began thinking systematically about it. I had already gained some basic insights into it and tested out some possible solutions before I began writing on it.

Our life with God, in meditation and prayer, is also vital here. For ultimately what we are looking for is a divine perspective upon these activities. Meditation enables us to perceive what lies in and through phenomena as opposed to merely looking at these with our eyes or our minds. We begin to see things as they really are, not just as they appear. We begin to view matters through God's eyes, not just at a nice objective distance. We begin to feel passionately about things, not just form conclusions about them. As Martin Thorton says, becoming a genuinely practical theologian involves not only "human understanding, intuitive insights and spiritual perception as well as learning," but also "prayer as mediator within the total theological scheme. . . . In this wide, deep sense prayer is the total experience of all things in Christ." Indeed, the intuitions and hunches which guide research and begin to provide answers "are unlikely to arise except under the influence of prayer." Also, detailed studies do not always lead to "a Q.E.D. solution to the problem, but at least to a personal hypothesis, or even a paradox, which can be made subject to contemplation."[16] A theology of everyday life that has insight and power must have a decidedly autobiographical and contemplative character.[17]

In addition, we need "full-time" theologians who have at least one foot firmly planted in the world. If you sense some vocation in this area, you could delay equipping yourself in a more formal sense until after you have experienced and reflected more on your work, family, and community involvement. If you are already involved professionally in theological work, you might step out from it for an extended period and work in a secular and nonacademic environment, perhaps even in some cases coming to see this as your permanent location. Or, as occasionally happens, you might combine part-time theological teaching with part-time but substantial involvement with people in serious need, as takes place with base communities in Latin America. Any of these moves would bring invaluable "qualifications" that no academic credentials can provide.

If you plan to study theology at an advanced level you could consider diverging from the usual research directions and format. As Martin Thornton notes:

> Our modern divinity faculties swarm with research students the results of whose studies will never be published and in many cases will never be read. I hopefully suggest that they would be better employed doing pastoral theology, regarded as an equal but separate discipline from scholarship. The results of such studies, demanding every bit as much intellectual application plus spiritual and imaginative insight, would I believe stand up better to the essential qualification for any worthy thesis: that of original thought.[18]

Certainly the outcome of such work would be deeply appreciated by many more Christians, especially if you drew their dilemmas, experience, and wisdom into your research. There are scores of everyday issues which as yet have received little or no formal theological scrutiny. Of course, it is not only research students but their teachers who need to revise their research and writing priorities.

Apart from the occasional non-technical book or denominational report, academic theologians more often write for their peers or their students than for the average Christian. Even their more popular efforts tend in both form and content to be dilutions of their more technical works. There are other forms of communication, such as dialogue, narrative, autobiography, as well as letters, parables, and workbooks. But how much have these been used? Having tried my hand at some of these in a small way I know how difficult it is. But we need writings of this kind and, as the work of C.S. Lewis and others demonstrates, if they are done well, they will be widely read.

But these proposals only refashion the current image of the theologian. What I said earlier about the fundamental role of images for our thinking has a particular application here. We need a new image of theology, not just a more informed and relevant theology, if we are to develop an effective understanding of everyday life.[19] We also need a new image of what it means to be a theologian. Democratizing theology so that it becomes the province of a larger population of Christians who are prepared to think about their faith in a coherent way is one aspect of this. But we need a new image of the "full-time" theologian as well. This is a vocation that some have. But from what I have said already, it is clear that academic credentials are no longer enough to qualify a person for this responsibility. As well as democratizing of theology, we need a deprofessionalizing of the theologian as well. This takes us further than any suggestions I have made so far.

We need "apostolic" theologians who will leave their desk and lectern for a more down-to-earth kind of life. While there are few theologians who do not practice what they preach in some measure, there are very few who are engaged in similar work, say, to someone like Paul. That is, in apologetic and evangelistic work, in church-planting and pastoring, in pioneering new models of education and training. The apostolic theologian, of which Paul was the first great exponent, places mission first and largely allows theological reflection to be generated by that. Learning goes on as people associate with him or her in that activity — observing, questioning, and imitating. There is no reason why many Christians cannot be involved with such a person and why many of their concerns cannot be dealt with in this setting. The trouble is that taking up the "apostolic" theological life entails a large drop in status and high degree of risk.

We also need a large number of what I like to term "barefoot" theologians. This is where those of you who are not professional theologians come back into the center of the picture. In many Third World countries there are insufficient doctors to cope with demands for medical help. Those trained to fill this gap have only an elementary medical training. Yet such people have been able to treat some 80 percent of the illnesses they confront. In a different area, Wycliffe Bible Translators have for decades successfully taken non-linguistically qualified people and given them the basic skills for translating the Bible into another language. I cannot think of any reason why the same principle cannot be followed in the theological area. All that is required is some familiarity with the major types of issues that might arise and certain skills in assisting others to work through those issues. Some of you are already relatively well self-trained in the theological area. Others have had some formal theological education. Much of the knowledge many theologians have gained, and other experiences they have had, is underemployed. Given some additional practical training, which would best come from someone who can model for them what they might do, they would be well placed to help other Christians develop a theology of everyday life. In fact, my guess is that the future of such a theology largely lies in their hands.

If we are to encourage a larger number of people to become "apostolic" or "barefoot" theologians, we cannot leave it to present theological institutions to produce them. Some of these institutions are beginning to break out of the traditional model of theological education, but they are still largely committed to it. Lay theological centers, most of which significantly have developed outside the main theological structures, are better placed to help, but many of them are also too influenced by the dominant model. Theological education by extension programs have some possibilities for overcoming the barrier, but these are still geared mainly to church-related ministries and emphasize some aspects of the learning process more than others. In addition to what all these can do, we require contemporary versions of the more practically-orientated and holistic "Paul-Timothy" type of theological training. Of themselves these may not be enough, but without them something vital will be lacking.[20]

Conclusion

So then, the call to develop a theology of everyday life that will aid in *redeeming the routines* in which we are engaged is in the long run a call to develop a new understanding and practice of theology itself. It is not just a call for theology to broaden its concerns, for theologians to enter a new field, or for theological colleges to fill out their curricula. Ultimately, it is a call to everyone involved in these to reexamine the model they are following and transform it into another. It is a call for a new form of theology and for new forms through which it may be expressed.

Nor is it just a plea to all Christians to become more aware of their dilemmas and responsibilities, to think more about the implications of their faith, to belong to more study groups and attend more courses. It is, fundamentally, a plea to reexamine what it means to be a Christian. It is a plea to develop a new vision and total style of life through which the reality of God may be expressed.

Questions for Reflection:

1. If it is true that theologians often "reside in a kind of ecclesiastical compound" (page 127), how does this affect their knowledge and vision?
2. Take one area of your life — economics, for example — and share with others the theology that lies behind your thoughts and ideas in that area.
3. Give an example of an ethical problem where the lay Christian is more likely to have expertise than the professional theologian.
4. How has your experience of life enabled you to "know" some theological point in the sense in which the author uses the term "know" on page 134?
5. "We are constantly in danger of overstressing the role of the intellect in our lives" (page 135). What aspects other than the intellect are important? Why are they important?
6. Take one of the doctrines discussed on pages 139 to 143 and show how it relates to your workplace and everyday routine.
7. How can you best equip yourself to be a theologian?

APPENDIX A
Lay Theology and Education Since 1945

Over the last few decades there has been a number of attempts to relate theology more closely to the world at the level of both ideas and practice. How far do these attempts take us into the everyday life of the average Christian? To the extent that they do, and do so effectively, we can build on them. I have made no effort to be exhaustive here, but rather sought to identify the main approaches. I have singled out three representative books, each of which came to my attention at an appropriate point in my own thinking or work. I have also discussed a number of representative institutions I have visited which attempt to take theology to a wider audience.

The First Steps

From World War II onward there was a growing interest in what was termed "the role of the laity" in both the church and the world. Some of this interest stemmed from gatherings, reports, and groups of the World Council of Churches. According to Hans Reudi-Weber, there were many reasons for this discovery:

It is partly due to the biblical and theological renewal which has revealed to us a new image of the church: the church as a people and a body, the church which is elected and sent for mission and service in God's world. The rediscovery also partly stems from our new world situation: the breakdown of the corpus Christianum; the processes of industrialization and secularization which tend to edge the church out of daily life into a religious ghetto; the fact that the church is becoming almost everywhere a minority which has great difficulty in communicating with the modern world. Wherever these new insights about the nature and task of the church and these challenges of the modern world are taken seriously—and the ecumenical movement attempts to do so—the question of the role of the laity immediately becomes prominent.[1]

During the same period, various major denominations were also rediscovering the importance of the laity. This was true in Roman Catholic as well as Protestant circles.[2] In part this was for similar reasons. But these denominations, and the congregations of which they were composed, felt some of the factors noted by Hans Reudi-Weber more directly. Some pastors and evangelists began to see the potential in their church members and devised ways of training them to be more effectively involved in congregational life. I can still remember the novelty of hearing about the courses and openings for church members set up by people like John Stott in England, or the programs and responsibilities arranged for Christians who were counselors at Billy Graham evangelistic crusades. Later the influence of fresh religious impulses upon the denominations led to greater involvement on the part of many church members. In the wake of the charismatic movement, this was true in the exercise of so-called spiritual gifts. Meanwhile, the radical discipleship movement led to a renewed interest in serving the community and confronting social and political issues. Local churches and denominations were also more directly aware of the declining number of people attending church, and this led to a variety of suggestions for mobilizing them or attracting them back to the fold. These ranged from new organizations within the congregation to full-scale stewardship schemes. Lay representation was also increased on denominational committees, conferences, and working groups; and there was a larger provision of chaplains to Christians in industry, universities, and other institutions.

This new mood was powerfully captured in a book published in 1958 by a well-known ecumenical missiologist, Hendrik Kraemer, entitled A Theology of the Laity.[3] This occasioned a great deal of interest and was reprinted several times in the next few years. In no other writing during that period was the role of the average Christian in both church and world argued so strongly and thoughtfully. I did not come across this book until some six or seven years after it was published. At that stage I was having increasing difficulties with the existence and consequences of the clergy-lay distinction in the church at large. I was also beginning to question the preoccupation in most local churches with filling their own buildings and organizations, rather than encouraging their members to fulfill their responsibilities as Christians in the wider community. When I finally got around to opening the book, I did not so much read it as devour it. It helped me realize just how introverted and one-sided most churches were and how much I myself had contributed to that. I could see how much they prevented those same laypeople from fully playing their part in the world as well.

In his book, Kraemer stressed the centrality of the layperson both in the church and in the world and pleaded that fuller theological attention be given to this. He insisted the role of the laity in both spheres had been regarded merely as an appendix to the doctrine of the church. Or, in the development of a Christian view of society, it had been treated too generally. He asked that the term "laity" include more than the elite nonclerical members of the church. It should embrace women and men, poor and wealthy, less-educated and well-educated, working class and middle class. What was required was not a theology of, but also for, the laity. To be effective, this had to be free from the technicalities of professional theology. It would only develop, he pointed out, through the cooperation of theologians and laypeople.

According to Kraemer, nothing less was required than a reversal in priorities. God's primary concern is for the world, not the church, and the church should reflect this in its own life. Although the church often claims that it exists on behalf of the world, in practice it is a highly introverted institution. The church must not only have missions or give service to the world, but become inherently a missionary and servant body. Christ embodied these two concerns in His own life and every layperson is required to imitate Him. This is not a matter of following an ethical example, but entering into a new way of life involving the whole person. Such a calling is as real as that of a missionary or an ordained minister and is in no way inferior to them. Here, said Kraemer, we have the starting point for a theology of the laity. He was not claiming to be saying anything new, but merely placing at the center of the doctrine and structures of the church something that till now had been relegated to the periphery.

Kraemer concluded that two major changes had to take place if a theology of the laity were to genuinely emerge. First, there must be a thoroughgoing revision of church structures. This includes the development of new forms of community such as house churches, in which the laity can really become the church. The laity must also have a greater share in preaching and leading worship at larger services. The church's activities must also be decentralized to cope with the mobility and diversity of modern life. Second, there should be a relocation of the place where dialogue between the church and the world occurs. Instead of this happening in church councils at a distance from the issues discussed, it should take place at existing meeting points where ordinary people work, live, and play. For it is through the laity, dispersed in the world, that this dialogue is already under way. If this dialogue is to be properly informed, it needs prayerful support, pastoral encouragement, and theological assistance.

For Kraemer also there was an indispensable complement to a theology of the laity. We needed "various theologies of the realities and spheres of the world," such as those of work, money, property, common life, and a personal and social ethics which addressed these issues.[4] Listening carefully to the world so that a genuine encounter with it takes place was crucial here. Only so would we discover the hidden points in the world which are the levers for social change. Actually contributing to the life of the world would express itself in a variety of ways, such as being certain kinds of people, undertaking disinterested service, becoming reconcilers in volatile conflicts, asking the hard questions which no one else is raising, and prophetically contradicting the world where necessary.

As I read this book I had a sense of mounting enthusiasm and challenge. So much has been written on this subject since, and so much of what Kraemer said has been taken for granted, that it is hard for me to recapture the freshness of the book's impact. But indicators of that impact are there in the book as I look at it again. Halfway through reading it I began to underline large sections of the text. Then I began to write check marks, scribble comments, and insert exclamations in the margin. The check marks multiplied and the comments became more and more affirmative the further I read. By these means I can retrace the upward curve of my excitement.

Kraemer's book crystalized the concerns underlying the formation of various institutions in Europe after World War II, beginning with the Evangelical Academy at Bad Boll in West Germany. These institutions sought to give laypeople a theological understanding of their responsibilities in church and world and to equip them better for service in both. Unlike seminaries and Bible schools, they focused mainly on people in secular employment and addressed issues relevant to their workaday lives. The academies also developed short, intensive courses of various kinds rather than full-time study programs.

My first encounter with one of these institutions was in the winter of 1968. I was studying in Switzerland at the time and a German friend took me to the Evangelical Academy at Mannedorf, not far from where we were living. This was quite unlike any institution I had visited in my own country. It had something of the atmosphere of a Christian conference center, yet was clearly a place where serious study and research took place. It was also frequented by many people who were not attenders of any church. The visit broadened my understanding of what could be done to assist Christians to relate their faith to life generally and to enhance the interchange between church and world.

The majority of these centers emerged in Western Europe. This was no accident, for the ravages of the Second World War left much to be done in the area of moral and social reconstruction. Many people, irrespective of their attitude to religion, wanted their societies to rebuild on a sound foundation. This was especially the case in Germany. Though these centers grew out of a particular social situation and took different forms in different countries, there was an underlying similarity in their goals, structures, and approaches.[5]

The evangelical academies in Germany from 1945 onward saw themselves as centers for discussion and research. Initially they drew together politicians, jurists, church administrators, and employees into two-week conferences so that they could discuss their specific concerns. In the following years conferences diversified. There were specific gatherings for different kinds of workers —

apprentices, master craftspeople, people in commerce, engineers, secretaries, and industrial leaders. Later on, attempts were made to bring all the different types of workers and levels of management in a single firm together. Operating through, and partly subsidized by industry and government, the academies issued their invitations to everyone in these groups, irrespective of their involvement in a church. The continuing State Church pattern in Germany aided this approach.

The academies also established special services to particular occupation groups. One such service attempted to draw teachers in elementary and secondary schools into conversations with church officials. Another concerned itself with labor questions and sought to create Christian cells in industry, form local workers' study groups, establish links between churches and labor, and make contact with the unions. The academies also developed links with other groups such as farmers. As well, there were courses for students wishing to enter journalism and conferences for editors at which religious, social, and cultural questions were discussed in the light of the Gospel. The academies also realized that some matters required more thorough study than was possible through these channels. This led to the creation of a network of university teachers who could contribute their expertise on particular issues. Questions discussed ranged from the role of Marxism in contemporary thought and life to social and vocational aspects of the life of the working woman.

In other parts of Europe centers developed that had much in common with the evangelical academies, but also differed from them. For example, the Iona Community in Scotland, composed of both ordained and non-ordained people united in a community of worship and work, grew out of the life of an intentional community. The Ecumenical Institute in Bossey, Switzerland sprang from the desire to draw laypeople and their concerns more fully into the work of the World Council of Churches. The Kerk in World movement in Holland set up a distinct sociological institute and established a center to equip church workers through nonformal training. Other organizations were set up in Sigtuna, Sweden, in Mannedorf, Switzerland and, with some difficulty, in various parts of the German Democratic Republic. In time, Roman Catholic centers developed in some of these countries. Here and there cooperation between Catholic and Protestant institutions also took place.

Unfortunately, the reliance upon academic resource people in many of these centers has tended to undermine their relevance and has also increased the expense involved in running them. Too great a reliance upon government subsidies has also at times interfered with the direction of their work. The emergence of independent, more specialized ministries to Christians in the workforce is also forcing these institutions to redefine their goals and activities. Most recently, cutbacks in government aid are requiring them to rationalize their operations and close some of their centers. So far as I can gather, they have also tended to focus increasingly upon ministers and churchgoers rather than aiming at broader participation.

It was not until later that organizations sharing some of the concerns of these centers arose outside Europe. These organizations have tended to lack the broad financial and secular backing that the European centers possessed and are less diverse in their operations. They include the Zadok Center in Canberra, Australia; the Shaftesbury Project in Nottingham, England; and the Center for the Study of Ethics and Social Policy, Berkeley, California. All of them are committed to developing a theology of the laity along the lines advocated by Kraemer. They provide resources for groups who wish to integrate faith and life. From time to time they hold workshops, seminars, and conferences for people in different occupations or who are concerned about particular issues. They also encourage the formation of vocational and other groups to think through such matters. Of course these are not the only institutions engaged in such activities, but they are among the most committed to it.

Some New Developments

During the last twenty years there have been some interesting developments in the area of what is described as "lay theology." Among books written on the issue is one by Richard Mouw entitled *Called to Holy Worldliness*.[6] This was written toward the end of the seventies out of its author's experience of many debates on the issue of lay responsibility to the Gospel.

What is particularly interesting about the book is the way it embodied the main shifts in emphasis that had taken place in developing a theology of the laity since the publication of

Kraemer's books just over twenty years before. For example, Mouw's background was the Christian college and he wrote as a layperson whose chief interest was social ethics. Mouw was also conscious of the need to go "beyond Kraemer" and viewed his work as forming "chapter two" of a theology of the laity. Therefore, he begins at the point at which Kraemer's book ends, that is he simply assumes that laypeople should take their full position in the church, develop a theological perspective upon their role in society, and find new ways of structuring and carrying out their responsibilities. He wishes to go further and be more specific about what a theology of the laity entails.

Mouw begins by noting the gap that still exists between theology and the corporate life of society – business, politics, education, and entertainment. He finds a similar gap between the concern for piety or evangelism on the one hand and the reality of social structures on the other. He does not regard the bridging of this gap as the only concern of laypeople and does not regard all laypeople as equally obligated to do something about it. But he does stress the need for more laypeople to become involved in this area. Although in his view the situation has improved since Kraemer wrote, there is still a need for extensive discussion of the role of the laity. This will happen if there is not only "a theology *of* the laity," to quote the title of Kraemer's book, but "a theology *for* the laity" and "a theology *by* the laity" as well.

A theology *of* the laity, he warns, involves more than thinking about who the laity are and what their calling is inside and outside the church. Such a topic could simply be appended to the themes of a systematic theology. Instead, the main subjects of such a theology – the doctrine of God, creation, humankind, salvation, church, sacraments, mission, and eschatology – should be reexamined for the implications they have for a theology of the laity. This is what John Macquarrie had begun to do by examining the relationship of the people with God, Christ, and the Spirit as well as their character, environment, and destiny.[7]

Out of this should come a theology *for* the laity. At this point Mouw moves quite beyond anything in Macquarrie's work. The agenda for such a theology would not be the clerically dominated concerns of traditional theological discussion, but the needs, dilemmas, and problems of laypeople themselves. The goal should be equipping the laity to fulfill their responsibilities and potential in the world. With the help of a range of biblical metaphors that describe various aspects of the life of the people of God, Mouw underlines the importance of every type of group and organization and every sphere of human life coming under practical theological scrutiny. But this will only take place if laypeople overcome their antipathy to theology—much of it well justified—and engage in a more relevant form of it themselves. For it is only laypeople who can help define the main issues that must be addressed and identify the key factors that must be taken into account.

So a theology must be developed *by* the laity as well. If they can develop a new model for their work and the skills to go with it, theologians can also contribute to this. The chief method by which Christians can gain clarity about their responsibilities is through "discernment." This enables us to identify the underlying motivations, dispositions, and forces at work in society as well as their personal, social, and cultural consequences. But discernment, insists Mouw, is essentially a communal act: intuitions, data, hypotheses, and proposals that come to laypeople from their experience of the world should be shared with the wider Christian community and weighed by it. Since God's presence in the world is a complex and hidden affair, however, insights that come out of this process must be regarded as tentative.

If discernment is the means by which laypeople come to understand their responsibility in the world, concern for those most disadvantaged by society should be the main focus of lay attention. The warrant for this concern is the special place the Bible accords to the "poor." Mouw has not only the economically poor in mind, but those who are discriminated against legally and politically. People that are significantly disadvantaged today are women and people of color, though many others are oppressed in some way. Such people may be affluent, privileged, and powerful, but still suffer oppression at other levels. Even if our main concern should be for those who are most disadvantaged, we cannot remain unconcerned about the plight of the more "well-off" members of society.

In his concluding chapter Mouw discusses ways in which people can be best equipped for ministry in the world. It is difficult, he says, to fulfill our role in the world and most people do not feel adequate to do it. There are no simple solutions and our effectiveness depends as much on personal renewal and growth as upon learning how to think and act rightly. Existing programs of lay education — adult Sunday School classes, senior fellowships, occupationally based Bible studies, Christian service organizations, and social action groups — go only part of the way here. These are meager in comparison with the resources available for the training of clergy. Lay education programs are often poorly staffed and planned. Educational goals are often subordinate to other purposes. The issues they discuss only rarely touch upon the role of laypeople in the world. Only if they are reconstituted could such structures equip laypeople more effectively.

During the last twenty years a number of organizations have emerged which embody the concerns expressed in Mouw's book. These organizations go beyond those that arose after World War II. Indeed, some of them go beyond Mouw's own recommendations. The centers described earlier mostly began in Europe, only later surfacing elsewhere. Their newer counterparts exist mostly in North America, but are now also emerging in other countries. Whereas the earlier centers received support from denominational, business, and government sources, the newer institutions have had to finance their operations primarily through fees and gifts. For that reason they sometimes have a more precarious existence than their predecessors. Another difference is that the newer institutions cater almost exclusively to Christians. These dissimilarities partly reflect the non-established church environment of most of the new enterprises, as well as their substantial lay origins.

It is encouraging to see that for the most part it was laypeople who established these new institutions. In one case this owed much to the Brethren connections of those involved. In another it was due to the Christian counter-culture environment in which the founders largely worked. Elsewhere laypeople coming out of a Reformed tradition, with its emphasis on Christ's rule over the whole of life, took the initiative. Unlike the evangelical academies and their later counterparts, these new centers also offer more substantial study programs. These programs take different forms in different institutions. Many require a graduate degree as an entrance requirement — and either have, or are seeking, academic accreditation. However, others cater to a broader audience and do not offer diplomas or degrees.

During the mid-eighties, during a twelve month period, I had the opportunity to visit a number of these institutions. This was not just a tourist exercise. I had learned from experience that the only way to really discern what was taking place was to spend an extended period of time in a place, taking part as fully as possible in its life and hearing the views of those at the grassroots as much as those at the top. Since then I have revisited these institutions, in some cases several times. Though it is difficult to convey their ethos and character in a paragraph or two, I would like to give a brief profile of the two most creative ones.

In Vancouver, Canada, Regent College occupies a striking new building on the edge of the University of British Columbia. The college began in the late sixties and offers programs ranging from a one year diploma to a four year Master's degree. With minor exceptions, all but the first program involve full-time study. The college also runs a summer school program open to anyone who is interested and has a number of extension courses. Begun as a deliberate attempt to take theology to the people, in terms of numbers Regent College has exceeded all expectations. It is now the largest theological institution anywhere in Canada. It has, in fact, increasingly developed into a kind of lay seminary. A significant proportion of its students hold down full-time jobs and undertake their programs part-time. A number of the courses, particularly in its intensive summer and winter offerings, focus on issues arising from home life, the wider culture, and the marketplace. Those students who will remain in the marketplace, or who choose to enter into it, are given opportunity to think through their vocational needs and direction.

In many respects, however, Regent College's curriculum, teaching methods, and form of assessment are mostly a modified version of that found in any theological college. What it does at this level it does very well indeed and many students have paid it glowing tributes. It continues to attract a very international clientele. But I wished there had been a more sustained attempt to rethink theological education for the whole people of God in terms of their everyday responsibilities and needs. It is indicative, perhaps, that the majority of the degree students seem to be looking for some type of full-time church-related work.

I have been fortunate enough to have two separate semester-length stays at New College, Berkeley as well as involvement in several intensive programs. This has been in existence for about fifteen years and rents accommodations from a theological college close to the Berkeley campus of the University of California. At the college, students can undertake a one year part-time diploma course or full-time Master's course in Christian studies, though the latter can also be completed part-time over a longer period. There is also a more intensive two year Master's program and there are certificate programs in both campus and cross-cultural ministry.

Any of the courses can be taken by people not pursuing a degree. To make courses more accessible, much of the teaching is conducted in the evenings, on weekends, or through intensive summer and winter courses. There are also extension programs for those living further afield. By far the majority of students at New College are part-time and expect to remain in a secular occupation. Here I experienced a far more communal atmosphere, observed a greater attempt to develop a new type of curriculum more directly related to the average Christian, and found a more concerted effort to help people integrate their growing theological understanding with the particular jobs, interests, and commitments they have.

How do these centers differ from more traditional theological institutions? Biblical studies courses are less technical. Historical studies give more attention to the effects of secularization on modern society and more on the effects of social, cultural, and multicultural concerns. Theological studies focus more on apologetics and on the doctrines of creation and the kingdom of God. More innovation is evident in, and more time is given to, Christian ethics. There are units on the formation of values, business and professional morality, the ethics of sex and family life, the problems of urban living, and contemporary economic and political issues. A greater range of interdisciplinary programs opens up a Christian perspective on such matters as world views, academic disciplines, art and society, the role of the media, and science and technology.

In the practical theology area, more room is given to such concerns as vocation, lay evangelism and spirituality, public discipleship, congregational leadership, and the role of women. Most of these institutions also organize weekend conferences on a variety of issues such as unemployment, power and powerlessness in the city, the Christian in the marketplace, faith and art, journal-keeping and life-planning, as well as specialized conferences for a broad range of occupational groups.

Some seminaries are now beginning to pay closer attention to a theology of, by, and for the people. In some cases this has developed through the work of Offices of Continuing Education attached to the seminary, as at Perkins School of Theology, Southern Methodist University, in Dallas. A highlight here is an annual Laity Week of lectures and workshops, though there are also moves to develop a concentration in the ministry of the laity in the regular teaching program. At Andover Newton Seminary near Boston, a center for the Ministry of the Laity servicing the outside community was established, from which a course has been developed for the seminary. A distinctive approach has been forged by Auburn Theological Seminary in New York. No longer a teaching institution, it has turned itself into a research and development center for the ministry of the laity that creates lay educational resources, tests them in congregations across the country, and then makes them available to whoever wants them.

More ambitious than any of these is the range of possibilities developed at Pittsburgh Theological Seminary, in conjunction with its Center for Business, Religion, and the Professions. Here dual Master's Degree programs in theology and law, business administration, public management, social work, information and library service, music, and health care administration can be undertaken in collaboration with Duquesne University, Carnegie-Mellon University, and the University of Pittsburgh. Building on a number of lay-oriented courses already offered in the School of Ministry, Fuller Theological Seminary now has a wide-range of courses and programs enabling students to focus on the ministry of the laity. Courses with this orientation are available in biblical studies, theology, and ethics with a focus on mutual ministry, Christian community, urban lifestyle, and theology of everyday life. In the ministry area there are courses on liberating the laity, influential lay thinkers, lay counseling and evangelism, equipping the laity, and popular culture. Degrees with a concentration on the ministry of the laity can now be undertaken and the way is being opened up to do advanced, even doctoral, work in this area. It is already possible to do Master's and Doctor's work in Psychology or Marriage and Family Therapy and Theology.

Such courses and programs aim to help those going into ordained or any church-related work to empower laypeople so that they can play their full part in both the church and the world. Since people coming to seminaries these days are increasingly diverse, many students are part-time or full-time in the marketplace, and in some cases not planning to leave it. Statistics show that a significant proportion of others who come into seminary looking to work in a congregation or Christian organization will end up in the marketplace anyway. Others will take up a tentmaking ministry of some kind, combining the ministry of ordinary work with some other specific form of ministry. Or they may seek ways of resourcing Christians in the marketplace, perhaps through becoming coordinators of lay ministry in congregations or more informally in workplace settings themselves.

Of course, there are many other institutions committed to bringing theology into closer contact with the world of the average Christian, a number of them outside North America. Some, like the Westwood Foundation in Los Angeles; the Institute of Christian Studies in Austin, Texas; as well as the Swiss Protestant Seminary in Aarau, Switzerland; and the Discipleship Training Center in Singapore, are more traditional in their interests or more focused on training for full-time Christian work. An organization that seeks to relate theology to life in a more informal and more ideological fashion is the L'Abri Fellowship, which now has centers in England, Holland, Sweden, and Switzerland, as well as the United States (where there are two sites—one in Massachusetts and one in Minnesota). At a post-graduate level an ambitious program is offered by the Institute for Christian Studies in Toronto, Canada, where faith is applied to contemporary world views, academic disciplines, and socio-political movements.

There are also a number of denominationally based resource and educational departments, for example, Ministry in Daily Life (Evangelical Lutheran Church in America), Ministry of the Laity in the Workplace (American Baptist Churches), and the Episcopal Church Center in New York. In one or two places there are Lay Academies attached to particular denominations, though these have tended to wane in support in recent years. There are other centers that aim to resource the laity through training events, consulting, publications, and research, such as the Alban Institute and the Cathedral College of the Laity, both of which are based in Washington. Such interdenominational and ecumenical organizations as Inter-Varsity Christian Fellowship's Marketplace Ministries and the Vesper Society, offer similar assistance. Many other organizations have a more specific or more local focus. Residential centers, such as the Mackenzie Study Center in Oregon and the C.S. Lewis Institute in Washington, also intermittently draw people together to reflect on a variety of concerns.

A Pioneering Approach

According to Richard Mouw, we are still in the second stage of the development of a lay theology. The third stage, he says, will involve the detailed discussion of specific problems. But there is more to the third stage than he suggests and moving into it will involve more novel approaches and institutions than have yet appeared. Still, attention is now beginning to be paid to specific aspects of work or nonwork life.

For example, books are starting to deal with such issues as professional ethics, living standards, the use of time and leisure. But there are many areas of daily life that have not yet even surfaced. We are also only beginning to see approaches to theological education which bring this to bear more closely on the everyday concerns of people.

In order to see what the future may hold in this area, we must look away from Europe and North America to the Two-thirds World. If it was in Europe that the first stage of a theology of the people came to the surface, and in North America that new developments in popular theological education first appeared, it is in the Two-thirds World that the move into a third stage is most advanced.

In recent years, theologians and educators in the West have turned their attention to this part of the world for two main reasons. Liberation Theology challenged them to redefine the content and method of what they were doing and Theological Education by Extension suggested a new model of training for ministry. Both these movements have opened up the possibility of a more effective translation of Christian convictions into everyday life situations.

Liberation Theology insists that the first step toward real understanding is to look closely at the situation in which we are placed. This situation has to be analyzed and all the factors that bear on it must be identified. So the concrete situation, not the biblical text, is the starting point for discerning what God wants of us in that situation. The Bible itself, they would claim, is a record of real people in real situations: it was as they actually confronted these and sought to understand them that God declared His purposes.

The trouble with most theology in the West was its failure to begin with concrete problems. This was why it was so rarely able to provide any concrete solutions. The widely talked about "irrelevance" of theology largely stems from this failure. Much of the writing that issued from Liberation Theology, at least in the initial stages, focused on the general economic, social, and political situation in Latin America and tended to be very academic in character. While it challenged the way in which theology was done in the West, it still reflected much of the Western style of communication. The people for whom it was written were mostly an educated elite. The setting in which much of it was done was primarily tertiary institutions. In other words such thinking was often more a theology of the people, rather than by and for the people.

One of the best known of the Liberation theologians, both inside and outside Latin America, is Jean Luis Segundo. I picked up his book, *The Liberation of Theology,* just a few months after I had made the decision to leave the academic world, yet before I had completed my time in it.[8] In a different setting than the Latin American one, I was also feeling my way toward a new model for doing theology. Segundo's book, which I read during a period when considerable pressure was coming my way to stay in the academic world, fell into my hands at the right time.

This is not to say that I always found myself in agreement with it. The illustrations of concrete situations contained in the book seemed too general, the reliance on Marxist analysis too heavy, and the style in which it was written too cerebral. But its criticism of the way in which theology has become so professionalized in the West, so confined to a select, well-educated audience and so vested with ecclesiastical interests, was penetrating. Contrast this, says Segundo, with the unprofessional, non-formal, and prophetic character of theology among Jesus and the early Christians. What we require is "the return of theology from the rarefied atmosphere of academia to the world of common sense." This "common sense" has little to do with the prepackaged "common sense" that is handed out to us through the mass media or in the commonplaces of the consumer society. Segundo lists four marks of such a "common-sense" theology:

1. We must move away from an abstract or academic theology to one which grows out of a commitment to change people and improve the world.

2. We must analyze how society works if we are to take the Word of God and convert it from a vague outline to a clearly defined message.

3. We must avoid stating purely timeless, universal truths and address God's Word to specific problems and situations.

4. We must not bend the Word of God to our own ends if we are to say something that is really creative and liberating.[9]

What this means in practice for the people of God is spelled out in Segundo's manual, *A Theology for Artisans of a New Humanity*.[10] In this he covers a number of the main themes of traditional theology, but in a way that is relevant to the situation of the church as community, the human condition, ideas of God, the meaning of the sacraments, and the notion of guilt. His work takes account of the major intellectual currents of the day and also the social and political situation in Latin America. Although Segundo does not examine the most common, day-to-day activities and concerns of such people, he does relate theology to the pressing social and political problems that they have.

The way in which the material in these volumes has been put together and used is interesting. There are a number of initial reflections interleaved with sections which develop and apply the central ideas more concretely and suggest topics for study. This material can be used in a number of ways, such as full-length courses, study weeks, and intensive seminars. It is the last of these formats which he and his colleagues have found most helpful for "busy laypeople." The latter are encouraged to take part in one seminar a year. This runs over three or four days and is broken up into four hourly sessions. Those attending are expected to participate fully in the brief periods sets aside for general questions, personal meditation, study groups, and group reports. The outcome should be a conversation and debate about what people have heard and about their real-life experiences. There is also time at each session for recollection and prayer.

I have discussed Segundo's approach in some detail for it is a vital part of his understanding of theology as a whole. One of the marks of the new stage in a theology of the people is its concern to find alternative ways of developing and disseminating it. However, Segundo's content and practice is mainly relevant to an educated elite. He also tends to begin from his understanding of the situation in which people find themselves rather than from their perception of it. In a more recent paper he admits this and talks about a shift in the work of some Liberation theologians which begins with the people and invites them to become more a part of the theologizing process.[11]

Part of the reason for this is that some theologians in Latin America have sought to identify much more with the beliefs as well as aspirations of the people, rather than tending to criticize many of these for their superficiality or even superstitious character. More significantly, a number of theologians began to move out of their seminaries for part of the time each year and work among the poorer classes. Here and there some of these thinkers have left the academic world behind altogether and placed themselves at the disposal of the poor and oppressed on the fringes of some of the great cities. This has led to a more people-orientated and people-involved approach to theology, perhaps even one that is too uncritical of certain aspects of the people's values and capacities.

Alongside these theological approaches, and in part overlapping them, there are two models of theological education coming out of the Two-thirds World which have a more grassroots flavor.

First, there is Theological Education by Extension or TEE. This does not draw people out of their local situation to train them for future service, but trains them for present service in their actual situation. By this means a greater number of people are able to be involved. With the help of specially prepared materials, these work alone or in groups, with regular visits by teachers.[12] But TEE is primarily geared to people who wish to exercise some ministry in the church. Also, both in content and method, much of it is merely a modified version of the residential theological college curriculum.

There are exceptions to this, such as some of the courses developed in Bangalore, India. Here, even in a course on Christology, students begin by studying the economic, social, and political setting in the first century and Jesus' response to it. Then they reflect on their own context and look for common elements between the two. As they let these two horizons interact, they open up a deeper understanding of both. Throughout the course, students work up a case study, evaluate some Christian activity, write their own parables, and carry out a practical project.[13]

Second, there is also the more informal learning that takes place in the so-called basic communities in the Two-thirds world.[14] This grass-roots church movement among the poor, particularly in Roman Catholic areas, has created small, lay-led communities which worship together and engage in social action. This provides a communal and practical setting in which ordinary people can learn to bring faith and life into real contact.

There are an estimated 150,000 of these in Central and Latin America. In the spirit of the Brazilian educator Paolo Freire, this involves identifying the actual situation in which disadvantaged members of society find themselves and then reflecting biblically on that situation. Out of this setting, with the help of itinerant "pastoral agents" who facilitate this process, have come materials that are more geared to the average person than those devised by Segundo. An interesting example of this from Peru has now been published in English.[15]

In these various ways—Segundo's seminars, TEE programs, and grass-roots church meetings—we begin to move beyond the second stage of a theology of the people. Each of these enters more fully and more effectively into the area that I have described as "the theology of everyday life." In these different settings, there is a real attempt to help people understand why that world is structured the way it is, how it affects their daily lives, and what, Christianly speaking, they can do about it. The people themselves are involved in the process of discovering these things and deciding how to respond to them.

In many respects our situation in the West is dissimilar. Everyday life has a different character, here and there is a higher level of education. It is important to recognize these differences. Otherwise a naive transfer of Two-thirds World models to Western conditions might be attempted. In any case the whole spirit of the Two-thirds World approach is against this. Its message is: begin with your own situation and allow the Word of God to come into contact with it. Since everyday reality for most people in the West is different to that in the Two-thirds World, the theology appropriate to our situation will in some respects be different as well.

In several Western societies, counterparts of the three Latin American approaches I have mentioned do exist. For example, the

Urban Theology Unit in Sheffield, England, has developed a methodology and program that borrows heavily from the Liberation Theology model. In doing so it has attracted a great deal of interest, but also provoked a significant degree of opposition. While it has challenged people's understanding of the concerns and methods of theology, it has carried over too much of the ideological superstructure and definition of the poor from the Two-thirds World. As a result, the Unit's work does not have as everyday a feel about it as it might.

TEE has now spread to many Western countries. In Australia, it has been taken up mainly by the Anglican General Board of Religious Education and the Diocese of Armidale, the Christian and Missionary Alliance churches and, most interestingly, at Nungalinya College, Darwin, Australia. The latter is a training institution for Aborigines sponsored by two leading denominations. Though it has a campus to which students come for part of their theological education — to help overcome the fragmentation of Aboriginal society by breaking down tribal barriers — most of the students' time is spent in their original tribal or urban settings. Through regular visits by college staff, help from local part-time tutors, the use of cassettes and highly innovative written materials, a real attempt is being made to relate theology to the actual situations, everyday problems, and indigenous aspirations of the Aboriginal people. The extensive use of "story" as a way of introducing students to the Bible, the incorporation of Aboriginal methods of learning, and the emphasis upon work alongside study in the local situation, result in a pioneering approach to theological education.

Over the last twenty years, in the United States, Australia, and Great Britain, grass-roots church communities have also come into being. There are modified versions of basic communities, mainly located in disadvantaged inner-city areas and often with a middle-class core.[16] While most of these arise within a particular denominational framework, links are often stronger with similar groups in the same area. Intentional communities in which both church and work join together also exist in many places: some of these are attached to a local church, others operate autonomously. Alternative churches — smaller, more informal, socially aware congregations meeting in basements or rented rooms — are also now a fact of life. House churches — whether independent, interdenominational, or based in a congregation—are also growing.

In all four types of grassroots communities, learning generally centers on the needs and desires of those involved or those whom they are seeking to reach. Concrete situations are frequently the starting point for biblical reflection, prayer, and discussion. Everyone participates in this process and learning is a holistic rather than head-orientated affair.

Conclusion

According to Ian Fraser, who has traveled widely and reported on recent trends at the grass-roots Christian level:

In much of the world church, the membership is no longer leaving theology to "theologians" but hammering it out at white heat in the fire of experience, tempering it as weaponry for the fights of life.

No longer is a prescribed, largely academic education looked to fit people for the task. The deficiencies of such an education are now being more and more recognized—the withdrawal from the mainstream of life; the lack of lively contact with the language and daily experience of so many people; the stress on book-knowledge; distance from a variously gifted and involved community in which to test and check insights. The theological training of Jesus, provided in the thick of life, which developed senses alert to the sights, sounds, smells, actions and interactions of life in the streets, in the homes and fields, on the lake; and which depended on wrestling in prayer and with the scriptures to find the mind of the Father, is being appreciated afresh. To training in theological awareness and perceptiveness of this kind, all sorts of people may have access. They are seizing their chance.

No longer is a scholarly caste given the last word in judging what is of worth in the field of theology—how can those sort out wheat from chaff who have never ploughed a field? Scholars can have a part in the whole work. They are no longer allowed to corner the theology market.

Illiterates now make perceptive contribution to the church's theological understanding. Work people on the land and in industry play their part in building up theological

resources. . . . At last theology is being done in community
by people with very diverse forms of experience. They provide an essential element which has been missing. Disciplined reflection, which theology requires, must have a richness of doing and perceiving to work on. . . . It takes a
community, reflecting deeply on reality as it is experienced,
to give theology substance and shape; a community in which
every member's contribution is respected and relished as
well as critically assessed that it might find its place in a
communal perceiving of God and his ways and works.[17]

But there is still a long way to go. What Fraser describes only
takes place among a small minority of Christians. In most places it
is business as usual. Where it does take place there is often too
academic a takeover of theological perspectives and too naive a
borrowing from non-Western grass roots models. These models,
and the theology that goes with them, are not sufficiently evaluat-
ed, corrected, and modified in the light of our particular situation
and other biblical principles. We need a home-grown approach
which has its own distinctive character.[18]

Appendix B
Resources and Agencies for Lay Education

(incorporating, with appreciation, *A Short List of Groups Concerned with the Ministry of the Laity,* by Edward A. White, April 1990)

If you wish to pursue any of the steps laid out in the last two chapters of this book, here are some suggestions.

1. If you are in a context which enables you to develop a clearer Christian perspective on everyday life, then your main need is for resources. You might begin by looking at the books in the endnotes to chapter 4 that are associated with the particular learning context you are in or at those in chapter 3 that are associated with the particular topic you are interested in. One of these may provide the starting point you require. For each country I have included a few key organizations in different regions, which could help you find out about others.

2. If you are looking for a particular context in which to build up a Christian understanding of everyday life, that is for one of the approaches listed in chapter 4, you could contact any one of the following. This list of lay resource centers is not exhaustive but does seek to include all the main agencies. It focuses more on national or regional centers than those which are purely local. The centers it identifies vary greatly, in purpose and approach as well as in theological and organizational allegiance.

Canada:

Institute for Christian Studies
229 College St.

Toronto, ON M5T 1R4
(416) 979-2331
A postgraduate school attracting Christians wishing to explore
the interconnections between theology and philosophy, social sciences, psychology, and art. Has a substantial publishing program
and a bi-monthly magazine *Perspective*. Also conducts seminars and
workshops in universities, colleges, and churches.

King-Bay Chaplaincy
Box 175, Room 204
Commercial Union Tower
Toronto-Dominion Center
Toronto, ON M5K 1H6
(416) 366-0818
An interchurch ministry to the business and professional community in the King-Bay area. Publishes *Journal of Lay Ministry* and
also has close connections with the Center for Ethics and Corporate Policy in Toronto, which helps businesses incorporate ethical
considerations into their operations.

Regent College
5800 University Blvd.
Vancouver, BC
V6T 2E4
(604) 224-3245
Offers graduate courses for laypeople who wish to study full-
time or part-time, though, also provides an ordination track. Intensive summer and winter programs also available. Extension centers operate in a number of cities in Western Canada and in
Seattle.

Workplace Ministry
P.O. Box 12034 Suite 2450
555 West Hastings Street
Vancouver, BC
V6B 4N4
(604) 682-3712
A congregationally based ministry to downtown businesses in
Vancouver.

United States:

The Alban Institute
4125 Nebraska Ave. N.W.
Washington, D.C. 20016
(202) 244-7320
Provides research, training events, consulting, and publications related to congregational and lay ministry development.

Auburn Theological Seminary
3041 Broadway
New York, NY 10027
(212) 662-4315
Specializes in field and other research on the ministry of the laity in daily life. Has developed a first-rate, three-year tested, manual for use in churches along these lines.

Career Impact Ministries
P.O. Box 5030
Arlington, TX 76011
(800) 4-IMPACT
Related to the Navigators, this evangelical group is concerned with providing resources that will help laity discern their vocation and carry out their ministry in the workplace.

Cathedral College of the Laity
South Tower
Washington Cathedral Mt. St. Alban N.W.
Washington, D.C. 20016
(202) 537-6562
Conducts research projects and develops models and materials to empower the ministry of the laity. Have done notable projects with retired persons and with business executives.

Center for Business, Religion, and the Professions
Pittsburgh Theological Seminary
616 North Highland Ave.
Pittsburgh, PA 15206-9980
(412) 362-5610
Offers forums on issues of public interest. Cooperative profes-

180 REDEEMING THE ROUTINESREDEEMING THE ROUTINES

sional Master's Degree programs between Pittsburgh Theological Seminary and Carnegie-Mellon University, Duquesne University, and the University of Pittsburgh enable students to earn dual degrees in theology, law, business administration, public management, social work, information and library science, music, and healthcare administration.

Center for the Ministry of the Laity
Andover-Newton Theological School
210 Herrick Rd.
Newton Center, MA 02159
(617) 964-1100, ext. 277
Produces workshops and publications for enabling lay ministry.

Christian Laity of Chicago
750 Green Bay Rd.
Winnetka, IL 60093
(708) 332-1146
An ecumenical organization which invites people to: celebrate God through Jesus Christ, grow in the Christian faith, experience supportive community, and develop unique gifts for service to others. Offers two-year institutes in Spiritual Companionship and in Small Group Development as well as a variety of workshops.

Christian Vocation Research Project
c/o Memorial Episcopal Church
1407 Bolton St.
Baltimore, MD 21217
(301) 669-0220
Discerning call in community; parish support for ministries; accountability for ministry.

CLAY (Clergy and Laity Together in Ministry)
5010 Six Forks Rd.
Raleigh, NC 27609
(919) 781-5197
Enabling the ministry of the laity in, through, and beyond the local congregation. Offers a range of courses and workshops to congregations on a fee basis.

Crossings
6337 Clayton Rd.
St. Louis, MO 63117
(314) 863-6381; 725-0801
Offers semester-long college accredited courses, weekend workshops, and a seminar in which people of faith share their secular callings and how they cross their faith in their daily life.

Doorways
4820 North 27th Place
Arlington, TX 22207
(703) 827-0336
An ecumenical team that offers consultation, training, and publications which help congregations strengthen spiritual community and ministry development. Also offers *Working from the Heart: Resources for Exploring Vocation*, materials, workshops, and an extended "Life Direction Lab."

Episcopal Church Center
615 Second Ave.
New York, NY 10017
(212) 867-8400
Publishes regular journal entitled *Ministry Development* and in other ways both encourages and resources mutual ministry in the church and the ministry of daily life.

Faith at Work
150 S. Washington St., #204
Falls Church, VA 22046
(703) 237-3426
A national network of leaders and learners involved in small group fellowships and new models of ministry. It publishes a magazine, holds regional conferences, and organizes leadership training and church renewal weekends.

Fellowship of Companies for
Christ International
2920 Brandywine Rd., #150
Atlanta, GA 30341
Brings together companies and businesspeople endeavoring to

operate overtly on Christian principles. Also releases videos and organizes seminars and conferences.

Foundation for Community Encouragement, Inc.
7616 Gleason Rd.
Knoxville, TN 37919
(615) 690-4334
   Influenced by the work of M. Scott Peck. Offers Community Building workshops and trains leaders to conduct such seminars. Committed to community building as a pathway to peace.

Fuller Theological Seminary
135 North Oakland
Pasadena, CA 91182
(818) 584-5200
   Provides a wide range of courses on life in the church and the world with a lay focus, as well as a degree program specializing in this. These are available in extension centers throughout the West as well. Also developing opportunity for postgraduate and doctoral work in lay ministry and theology.

Institute for Christian Studies
1909 University Ave.
Austin, TX 78705
(512) 476-2772
   Provides range of undergraduate classes in theology for students and general public, hosts annual seminars and conferences, and is now moving into graduate theological education.

The Institute for Servant Leadership
P.O. Box 1081
Hendersonville, NC 28793
(704) 697-6957
   Offers courses and workshops on the power of servant leadership.

Kogodus
Montana Synod Office Building
2415 13th Ave.

Great Falls, MT 59405
(405) 453-1462
A movement of Christian renewal, offering events, usually in weekend retreat settings, based on Luther's Small Catechism. These events encourage and equip participants for service and caring by using the gifts and talents God has given them. Beyond the basic course, "Faith & Life," are courses adapted to specific ministries such as in prison settings and for caregiving families.

Laity Lodge
P.O. Box 670
Kerrville, TX 78029-0670
(512) 896-2502
A retreat center with a laity library and cassette carrels for the purpose of helping ordinary believers deepen their Christian commitment and discover their ministry in the church and world.

Laynet
5908 Nevada Ave. N.W.
Washington, D.C. 20015
(202) 362-0541
Offers workshops and retreats on the issues of lay ministry and the role of the church in a culture that is disintegrating politically, economically, morally, and spiritually.

Links: Lay Academy
Moravian Biblical Seminary
West Locust St.
Bethlehem, PA 18018
(215) 861-1519
Provides a meeting point for concerns in the church and the world and seeks to equip laypeople for their roles in congregations and society.

The Lutheran Academy
6006 West Wisconsin Ave.
Wauwatosa, WI 53213
(414) 774-8558
Provides an arena for dialogue, study, and debate where persons

can explore ways to deal with occupational and societal issues of the day within the context of theological perspectives. Offers conferences around the country in which all aspects of the issues are discussed.

Marketplace Ministries
6400 Schroeder Rd.
P.O. Box 7895
Madison, WI 53707-7895
(608) 274-9001
A project of Inter-Varsity Christian Fellowship to enable people to be faithful disciples in the workplace. Provides the newsletter *Networks,* and videotapes, as well as a radio ministry. It is currently developing the *Marketplace Study Bible.*

Ministry in Daily Life
Evangelical Lutheran Church in America
8765 W. Higgins Rd.
Chicago, IL 60631-4195
(312) 380-2870
Provide a wide variety of resources to encourage and support the ministry of the laity.

Ministry of Money
2 Professional Drive, #220
Gaithersburg, MD 20879
(301) 670-9606
Focuses on growth in discipleship, compassion for the poor, and global stewardship. This takes place through basic and advanced workshops, immersion experiences in Third World countries, and other events.

Ministry of the Laity in the Workplace
American Baptist Churches
P.O. Box 851
Valley Forge, PA 19482-0851
(215) 768-2412
This group, like the preceding, supplies a range of resources relating to the ministry of the laity.

The National Center for the Laity
1 East Superior St.
Chicago, IL 60611
(312) 271-0289
  Publishes the newsletter *Initiatives,* as well as a variety of other publications to facilitate the ministry of the laity, especially within the Roman Catholic Church.

New College Berkeley
2606 Dwight Way
Berkeley, CA 94704
(415) 841-9386
  A graduate school of Christian and interdisciplinary studies for laypeople. Offers Master of Arts degrees in Christian Studies and in Theology, available through evening, weekend, and summer or winter intensive classes.

New Ministries: New Models for Ministry
1102 Stannage Ave.
Albany, CA 94706
  New Models for Ministry seeks to assist Christians as they discover, nurture, and celebrate their ministry as the people of God in everyday life — at work, home, and in the community. Publishes the newsletter *New Ministries.*

Pastoral Care Services
7312 Portland Ave.
Minneapolis, MN
(612) 866-4055; 423-2449
  Through seminars, consultations, written literature, and video equipping materials, helps churches to prepare their members for the provision of pastoral care in their congregations.

Savannah Presbytery "School of the Laity"
P.O. Box 880
Brunswick, GA 31521-0880
(912) 264-1997
  A two year program of lay training involving 306 hours of study including Bible, theology, ministry, history, mission, polity, and ethical decision-making.

The Servant Institute
1519 Western Ave.
Glendale, California 91201
(818) 246-9842
Developing a curriculum and library of resources on servant leadership.

The Servant Leadership School
1640 Columbia Road N.W.
Washington, D.C. 20009
(202) 328-7312
An affiliate of the Church of the Savior. Offers classes, seminars, and workshops. Special concern for teaching people to work with the underprivileged.

The Servant Society
Valle Verde #D-502
900 Valle de los Amigos
Santa Barbara, CA 93105
A coalition of people dedicated to the promotion of servant leadership.

Stephen Ministries
1325 Boland
St. Louis, MO 63117
(314) 645-5511
Provides a year-long training course and a variety of workshops and conferences for people wishing to move into lay caring and counseling in and around their congregations.

Strategic Careers Project
1284 Mica Lane
Colorado Springs, CO 80906
(719) 471-9191
Assists marketplace Christians and others considering a change in vocation to identify and move into occupations where a Christian presence is most needed in our society at present.

The Vesper Society
311 MacArthur Blvd.

APPENDIX B

San Leandro, CA 94577
(415) 633-0666
Dedicated to helping individuals and organizations throughout the world increase their capabilities for service, especially to the underserved, and to emphasizing the relationship of moral and ethical values to the structures of society. Publishes *Laity Exchange*.

Apart from these lay institutes, there are other organizations which set up occasional short courses or lecture series as part of a broader program. These may be attached to colleges, universities, parachurch organizations, grass-roots communities, or local churches. For example, throughout North America, Christian liberal arts colleges provide, with varying degrees of specificity, an institutional context for relating faith to everyday life and information about these can be obtained from:

The Christian College Coalition
235 Second Street, N.E.
Washington, D.C. 20002

If you are seeking materials for a group you wish to commence or in which you are involved, or a resource person to assist you in dealing with a particular topic, apart from the organizations listed above, you could contact the relevant departments of lay and adult education in your own denomination.

Endnotes

Chapter 1: Setting the Scene

1. J. Baillie, *Christian Devotion* (New York: Oxford Univ. Pr., 1962), 70.
2. C. Eastwood, *The Priesthood of All Believers* (London: Epworth, 1960), 238.
3. M. Gibbs, *Christians with Secular Power* (Minneapolis: Fortress, 1981), 36.
4. E. Brunner, *The Misunderstanding of the Church* (London: Lutterworth, 1952), 50.
5. The most detailed survey of the rise of the clerical/lay distinction is that of the Roman Catholic scholar A. Faivre, *The Emergence of the Laity in the Early Church* (Mahwah, N.J.: Paulist, 1990). His opening chapter, on the New Testament, is entitled: "The Wonderful Time When There Was Neither Clergy Nor Laity."
6. F. Buechner, *The Sacred Journey* (New York: Harper & Row, 1982), 1-2; see also his *Now and Then* (New York: Harper & Row, 1983); and *Alphabet of Grace* (New York: Harper & Row, 1970).
7. P.J. Palmer, *The Company of Strangers: Christians and the Renewal of Public Life in America* (New York: Crossroad, 1981), 39-40.
8. P.J. Palmer, *The Active Life: A Spirituality of Work, Creativity, and Caring* (New York: Harper & Row, 1990).
9. C. Cummings, *The Mystery of the Ordinary* (New York: Harper & Row, 1982), ix.
10. Of the growing number of more popular books—generally written by laypeople—arguing that the ordinary Christians should be given their proper due and that theological reflection should be an integral part of their lives, see especially R. Paul, *Liberating the Laity: Equipping All the Saints for Ministry* (Downers Grove, Ill.: InterVarsity, 1985); A. Rowthorn, *The Liberation of the Laity* (Wilton, Conn.: Morehouse-Barlow, 1986); and D.R. Leckey, *Laity Stirring in the Church: Prophetic Questions* (Minneapolis: Fortress,1987). More denominational in focus are J.D. and E.E. Whitehead, *The Emerging Laity: Returning Leadership to the Community of Faith* (New York: Doubleday, 1986); F.H. Thompsett, *We Are Theologians: Strengthening the People of the Episcopal Church* (Cambridge, Mass.: Cowley, 1989); and W.E. Rademacher, *Lay Ministry: A Theological, Spiritual, and Pastoral Handbook* (New York: Crossroad, 1991).

11. J. Ellul, *The Presence of the Kingdom*, 2nd. ed. (Colorado Springs: Helmers & Howard, 1989), 115–16.

Chapter 2: The Credibility Gap

1. One of the better examples of the former, itself written by a layman, was the small book by H.J. Schulz, *Conversion to the World: Perspectives for the Church of Tomorrow* (London: SCM, 1967). See especially the section of "Migration to Real Life" (p. 93ff). For a perceptive appraisal of the strengths and weaknesses of the second, see A. Dumas, *Political Theology and the Life of the Church* (London: SCM, 1978).

2. The most sensitive treatment of this whole approach is provided by R.J. Schreiter, *Constructing Local Theologies* (Maryknoll, N.Y.: Orbis, 1985). From the anthropological side see especially C. Kraft, *Christianity in Culture* (Maryknoll, N.Y.: Orbis 1979).

3. The most accessible introduction to a story and character-oriented approach to ethics is provided by the writings of S. Hauerwas, beginning with his collection *Vision and Virtue: Essays in Christian Ethical Reflection* (Notre Dame, Ind.: Univ. of Notre Dame Pr., 1974). The main philosophical justification is still that of A. MacIntyre, *After Virtue: A Study in Moral Theory*, 2nd ed. (Notre Dame, Ind.: Univ. of Notre Dame Pr., 1984).

4. The most extensive discussion of this general area comes in the recent book by D.S. Browning, *A Fundamental Practical Theology: Descriptive and Strategic Proposals* (Minneapolis: Fortress, 1991).

5. On the first, see the helpful if limited treatment by N. Pittenger, *The Ministry of All Christians: A Theology of Lay Ministry* (Wilton, Conn.: Morehouse-Barlow, 1983); as well as R. Benne, *Ordinary Saints: An Introduction to the Christian Life* (Minneapolis: Fortress, 1988). On the second, see the revealing article by J.L. Segundo, "Two Theologies of Liberation," in *Liberation Theology: A Documentary History*, ed. A. Hennelly (Maryknoll, N.Y.: Orbis, 1990); and now the comparative approach developed by W. Dyrness, *Invitation to Cross-Cultural Theology: Case Studies in Vernacular Theology* (Grand Rapids: Zondervan, 1992).

6. W. Diehl, *Christianity and the Real Life* (Minneapolis: Fortress, 1976), v.

7. See further the results of the multi-denominational Survey on Religion and Daily Life conducted by the Search Institute, Minneapolis (available from 122 West Franklin, #525, Minneapolis, MN 55404). Also, with a narrower focus, the similar findings of the Congregations and Business Life Project, *Faith and Work: Personal Needs and Congregational Responses*, The Center for Ethics and Corporate Policy, Chicago, 1991.

8. H. Thielicke, *The Trouble with the Church* (Grand Rapids: Baker, 1965), 76.

9. W. Diehl, *Christianity and Real Life*, v-vi.

10. H. Thielicke, *The Trouble*, 81.

11. M. Thornton, *The Function of Theology* (London: Hodder and Stoughton, 1968).

12. D.E. Wingeier, *Working Out Your Own Beliefs: A Guide for Doing Your Own Theology* (Nashville: Abingdon, 1980), 17–18.

13. Ibid.

14. Outside specifically Christian circles, authors from a range of disciplines have given increasing attention to the importance of everyday life, among them E. Goffman, *Presentation of Self in Everyday Life* (Woodstock, Anchor, 1976), from a psychological perspective; A. Schutz, *Collected Papers*, vol. 1–2 (The Hague, Netherlands: Martinus Nijhoff, 1962); and from a cultural studies vantage point, M.

deCertau, *The Practice of Everyday Life* (Berkeley, Calif.: Univ. of California Pr., 1984).

Chapter 3: The Texture of Daily Life

1. On this whole area see further my book, *The Tyranny of Time* (Downers Grove, Ill.: InterVarsity, 1983).
2. One who opens up this subject is J. McInnes, *The New Pilgrims* (Sydney, Australia: Albatross, 1980).
3. But see further I. Illich, *Energy and Equity: Toward a History of Needs:* (New York: Pantheon, 1978).
4. Among others see the composite work by the American Friends Committee, *Taking Charge: Achieving Personal and Political Change Through Simple Living* (New York: Bantam, 1977); the collection of articles by R.J. Sider, ed., *Living More Simply: Biblical Principles and Practical Models* (London: Hodder and Stoughton, 1980); and J.F. Kavanaugh, *Following Christ in a Consumer Society*, 2nd. ed. (Maryknoll, N.Y.: Orbis, 1991).
5. "Baby Boomers in the Church: Different Generation, Different Needs," *Twin Cities Christian*, 3 September 1992.
6. See especially the essays on "Shopping World: The Palace of Modern Consumption" and "The Fur Hate" in J. Carroll, *Sceptical Sociology* (London: Routledge and Kegan Paul, 1980).
7. On this area generally one of the most practical places to begin is G. Tucker, *The Faith-Work Connection: A Practical Application of Christian Values in the Marketplace* (Toronto: Anglican Book Center, 1987). See also, for small group discussion purposes, E. Wakin, *Monday Morality: Right and Wrong in Daily Life* (Mahwah, N.J.: Paulist, 1980); and R. Banks and G. Preece, *Getting the Job Done Right: Eight Sessions on Developing a Christian Perspective on Work* (Wheaton, Ill.: Victor, 1992).
8. On some of these issues see P. Marshall et al., *Labour of Love: Essays on Work* (Toronto: Wedge, 1980); C. Redekop and U.A. Bender, *Who Am I? What Am I?: Searching for Meaning in Your Work* (Grand Rapids: Academie/Zondervan, 1988); L. Hardy, *The Fabric of This World: Inquiries into Calling, Career Choice and the Design of Human Work* (Grand Rapids: Eerdmans, 1990); and more systematic in approach, M. Volf, *Work in the Spirit: Toward a Theology of Work* (New York: Oxford Univ. Pr., 1991).
9. T. Slater, *The Temporary Community* (Sydney, Australia: Albatross, 1984) on camping.
10. R.K. Johnston, *The Christian at Play* (Grand Rapids: Eerdmans, 1983), discusses certain approaches to leisure in a helpful way. So too does L. Ryken, *Work and Leisure in Christian Perspective* (Portland, Ore.: Multnomah, 1987); and now L. Doohan, *Leisure: A Spiritual Need* (Notre Dame, Ind.: Ave Maria, 1990).
11. An excellent starting point is, of course, Robert Bellah et al., *Habits of the Heart* (New York: Harper & Row, 1986). Less profound but revealing are J. Patterson and P. Kim, *The Day America Told the Truth: What People Really Believe about Everything That Really Matters* (New York: Prenctice-Hall, 1991); and G. Barna, *What Americans Believe: An Annual Survey of Values and Religious Views in the United States* (Glendale, Calif.: Regal, 1992).
12. See H. Mol, et al. *Western Religion: A Country by Country Sociological Survey* (The Hague, Netherlands: Mouton, 1972).
13. See again Banks, *Tyranny of Time*, 1983. See especially for the American context, M. O'Malley, *Keeping Watch: A History of American Time* (New York:

Penguin, 1990); and, more broadly, J. Rifkin, *Time Wars: The Primary Conflicts in Human History* (New York: Henry Holt, 1987).
14. For example by D. Lyon, *The Information Society: Issues and Illusions* (Oxford, Great Britain: Polity, 1988); and A. Emerson & C. Forbes, *The Invasion of the Computer Culture* (Downers Grove, Ill.:InterVarsity, 1989). More generally see J.D. Bolter, *Turing's Man: Western Culture in the Computer Age* (Chapel Hill, N.C.: Univ. of North Carolina Pr., 1984).
15. Ellul, *Presence of the Kingdom*, 145–48.

Chapter Four: The Reality Principle

1. For further information see R. and J. Banks, *The Church Comes Home: A New Base for Community and Mission* (Sydney, Australia: Albatross, 1989), especially chapter 10. Among the increasing number of books on this phenomenon see also L. Barrett, *Building The House Church* (Scottsdale, Pa.: Herald, 1986); B.J. Lee and M.A. Cowan, *Dangerous Memories: House Churches and Our American Story* (Kansas City, Mo.: Sheed and Ward, 1986); and C. Smith, *Going to the Root: 9 Proposals for Radical Church Renewal* (Scottsdale, Pa.: Herald, 1992).
2. Diehl, *Christianity and Real Life*, 97ff.
3. There is a brief discussion of the importance of modeling learning in L.O. Richards, *A Theology of Christian Education* (Grand Rapids: Zondervan, 1975), 30–50, 80–87. Further on this topic see J.R. Clinton and P.D. Stanley, *Connecting: The Mentoring Relationships You Need to Succeed in Life* (Colorado Springs: NavPress, 1992).
4. See further R. Banks, ed., *Private Values and Public Policy: The Ethics of Decision-making in Government Administration* (Sydney: Anzea, 1983), especially the introduction which describes the process followed. For an American approach to some of the same issues, containing some similarities in approach, see J.C. Haughey, ed., *Personal Values in Public Policy: Essays and Conversations on Government Discernment* (Mahwah, N.J.: Paulist, 1979).
5. I. Fraser, *Reinventing Theology As People's Work* (London: USPG), 61–65.
6. T. Groome, *Christian Religious Education* (New York: Harper & Row, 1980), 157–62.
7. Fraser, *Reinventing Theology*, 39.
8. See D.E. Wingeier, *Working Out Your Own Beliefs: A Guide for Doing Your Own Theology* (Nashville: Abingdon, 1980).
9. Quoted in Fraser, *Reinventing Theology*, 56–60. For a related approach see W. Wink, *Transforming Bible Study* (Philadelphia: Fortress, 1973).
10. See R. Banks, *Going to Church in the First Century*, 2nd ed. (Auburn, Maine: Christian Books, 1980).
11. John Macquarrie, *The Faith of the People of God: A Lay Theology* (London: SCM, 1972), 4.

Chapter Five: A People's Theology

1. Though it only came into my hands some time after I had completed this book, the general approach outlined in the following pages has much in common with that spelled out by L. Green, *Let's Do Theology: A Pastoral Cycle Resource Book* (London: Mowbray, 1990) and exemplified in his earlier account, *Power to the Powerless: Theology Brought to Life* (London: Marshall Pickering, 1987). The main difference would be the more normative place I accord the Bible, though I would want to see what it has to offer worked out in dialogue with concrete

situations not just applied unilaterally to them.

2. B. Wilson, "Notes Towards a Theology of Everyday Life," *St. Mark's Review* 126 (1986): 17.

3. G. Hughes, "Every Man a Theologian," *Interchange* 18 (1976): 121.

4. See further the preface to my book, *Paul's Idea of Community: The Early Home Churches in their Historical Setting* (Grand Rapids: Eerdmans, 1987).

5. Banks, *The Church Comes Home*, 1989.

6. N. Carr, "The Social Impact of Christian Theology and Pedagogy," *The Journal of Christian Education* 86 (1986): 24.

7. R. Broholm, "Envisioning and Equipping the Saints for Change," in *The Laity in Ministry: The Whole People of God for the Whole World*, ed. G. Peck and J.S. Hoffman (Valley Forge, Pa.: Judson), 131–33

8. See especially here the work of S. Hauerwas, *A Community of Character: Toward a Constructive Christian Social Ethic* (Notre Dame, Ind.: Univ. of Notre Dame Pr., 1981); and, with particular reference to the theme of their book, J.D. Anderson and E.E. Jones, *Ministry of the Laity* (New York: Harper & Row, 1986).

9. As well as Brother Lawrence's well-known book *The Practice of the Presence of God* (various publishers), there is the down-to-earth approach endorsed by E. Underhill, *The Spiritual Life* (Wilton, Conn.: Morehouse, 1955). See especially part 3.

10. As earlier, Palmer, *The Active Life*.

11. See, for example, T. Howard, *Hallowed Be This House* (Harrison, N.Y.: Ignatius, 1979); and E. Boyer, *Finding God at Home: Family Life as Spiritual Discipline* (New York: Harper & Row, 1988).

12. See J.C. Haughey, *Converting 9 to 5: A Spirituality of Daily Work* (New York: Crossroad, 1989); and W. Diehl, *The Monday Connection: A Spirituality of Competence, Affirmation, and Support in the Workplace* (New York: Harper & Row, 1991).

13. A work affirming the fundamental place of ethics for doctrine is J.W. McClendon, Jr., *Systematic Theology: Ethics* (Nashville: Abingdon, 1986).

14. See P. Marshall, "Dying and Rising with Christ: Theology for a Modern World," *Zadok Papers*, series 2, 1986.

15. On this generally, see A. Holmes, *All Truth Is God's Truth* (Grand Rapids: Eerdmans, 1977); and B.J. Walsh and J.R. Middleton, *The Transforming Vision: Shaping a Christian World View* (Downers Grove, Ill.: InterVarsity, 1984).

16. M. Thornton, *Function of Theology*, 69, 72.

17. The theologian who has most used an autobiographical approach, if at times in too subjective a manner, is Harvey Cox. See, for example, his book *Religion and the Secular City* (New York: Simon and Schuster, 1984). A model of meditative theological reflection, which also has a genuine feel for concrete reality, is the classic book by J.V. Taylor, *The Go-Between God: The Holy Spirit and the Christian Mission* (Philadelphia: Westminster, 1972).

18. M. Thornton, *Function of Theology*, 123.

19. Some moves in this direction may be found in E. Farley, *Theologia: The Fragmentation and Unity of Theological Education* (Minneapolis: Fortress, 1983); and M. Stackhouse, *Apologia: Contextualization, Globalization, and Mission in Theological Education* (Grand Rapids: Eerdmans, 1988). Also now B. Wheeler and E. Farley, eds., *Shifting Boundaries: Contextual Approaches to the Structure of Theological Education* (Louisville: Westminster/John Knox: 1991).

20. Though he is addressing the issue of Christian education more generally, helpful clues to the way learning should take place in such training may be found in P.J. Palmer, *To Know As We Are Known: A Spirituality of Education* (New York: Harper & Row, 1983).

Appendix A

1. H.R. Weber, "The Rediscovery of the Laity in the Ecumenical Movement," in *The Layman in Christian History*, ed. S. Neill and H.R. Weber (London: SCM, 1963), 379–80.
2. Y. Congar, *Lay People in the Church: A Study for a Theology of the Laity*, 2nd ed. (London: Chapman, 1964).
3. H. Kraemer, *The Theology of the Laity* (London: Lutterworth, 1958).
4. Ibid., 185.
5. On these and other possibilities for lay education made during this period see M. Gibbs and T.R. Morton, *God's Lively People: Christians in Tomorrow's World* (London: Fontana, 1971).
6. R. Mouw, *Called to Holy Worldliness* (Minneapolis: Fortress, 1980).
7. See again J. Macquarrie, *The Faith of the People of God: A Lay Theology* (London: SCM, 1972). Compare the approaches of E. Farley, "Interpreting Situations" and O.S. Browning, "Practical Theology and Religious Education," in *Formation and Reflection: The Promise of Practical Theology*, ed. L.S. Mudge and J.N. Poling (Minneapolis: Fortress, 1987), 11–14, 88–92.
8. J.L. Segundo, *The Liberation of Theology* (Maryknoll, N.Y.: Orbis, 1976).
9. Ibid., 39.
10. J.L. Segundo, *A Theology for Artisans of a New Humanity* (Maryknoll, N.Y.: Orbis, 1974).
11. J.L. Segundo, "Two Theologies of Liberation," in *Liberation Theology: A Documentary History*, ed. A. Hennelly (Maryknoll, N.Y.: Orbis, 1990).
12. For further information on TEE in Latin America see K.B. Mulholland, *Adventures in Training in the Ministry* (Phillipsburg, N.J.: Presbyterian & Reformed, 1976).
13. Details of this course are available from C. Sugden, Oxford Center for Mission Studies, P.O. Box 70, Oxford, UK.
14. See the exhaustive and perceptive analysis by G. Cook, *The Expectation of the Poor: A Protestant Perspective on Base Ecclesial Communities* (Maryknoll, N.Y.: Orbis, 1986).
15. For an example of this educational process at work among poorer groups, see V. Caminando, *A Peruvian Catechism* (London: SCM, 1985) or E. Cardenal, *The Gospel in Soltiname* (Maryknoll, N.Y.: Orbis, 4 volumes, 1978–1982).
16. For a survey of some of the main communities still operating in North America, see the recent article, "Jesus' People," *Christianity Today* 14 September 1992, 19–25.
17. Fraser, *Reinventing Theology*, 4–5.
18. For a recent report on emerging forms of theological reflection, primarily in developing countries, see S. Amirtham and J.S. Pobee, eds., *Theology by the People: Reflections on Doing Theology in Community* (New York: World Council of Churches, 1986). The discussion of their implications for theological reflection in developed countries shows how much remains to be done to biblically critique this, to contextualize what is valuable, and to translate it into grass-roots educational structures. Relevant to this whole question, though not written from a Christian perspective, is the attempt to relate the work of Paolo Freire to ordinary life in I. Shor, *Critical Teaching and Everyday Life* (Chicago: Univ. of Chicago Pr., 1987).